Handbook

QUILOMBISMO

HKW

O Quilombismo

Of Resisting
and Insisting.

Of Flight as Fight.

Of Other
Democratic
Egalitarian
Political
Philosophies

Where do we find such experience? In the Quilombos. Quilombo does not mean escaped slave, as the conventional definitions say. It means fraternal and free reunion, or encounter; solidarity, living together, existential communion. Quilombist society represents an advanced stage in sociopolitical and human progress in terms of economic egalitarianism. Known historical precedents confirm this position. As an economic system, Quilombismo has meant the adaptation of African traditions of communitarianism and/or Ujamaa to the Brazilian environment. In such a system, relations of production differ basically from those that prevail in the capitalist economy, based on the exploitation and social degradation of work, founded on the concept of profit at any human cost, particularly the cost of the lives of enslaved Africans. Quilombismo articulates the diverse levels of collective life whose dialectic interaction proposes complete fulfillment and realization of the creative capacities of the human being. All basic factors and elements of the economy are of collective ownership and use. Work is not defined as a form of punishment, oppression or exploitation; work is first a form of human liberation, which the citizen enjoys as a right and a social obligation.

—Abdias Nascimento, 'Quilombismo: An Afro-Brazilian Political Alternative'[1]

This text is an abridged version of a contribution to the *O Quilombismo Reader*, the publication accompanying the project. For further information see p. 278.

1 Abdias Nascimento, 'Quilombismo: An Afro-Brazilian Political Alternative', *Journal of Black Studies* 11/2 (December 1980), 141–178.

> Each return, Symbolic and actual, was a great blow in the great cultural task of revolution... Each escape, each flight was a species of marronage, the quest for a free space from where to wage the ongoing process of revolt against the cultural colonization carried out by the productive bourgeoisie who attempted to model America in its own image.
>
> —Sylvia Wynter, 'Black Metamorphosis: New Natives in a New World'[2]

There are manifold entries into this spiral of a story, the story of *quilombismo*. This ever-unfolding story whose beginnings and ends are regenerative. Like ecdysis—the process of a snake shedding its skin during growth—the story refuses to have one shell, one skin, one container, but renews its clothing when necessary. With the shedding of its skin, the story always has the potential for a new beginning and end, as it literally refreshes, recalibrates, rehabilitates itself, and rejuvenates.

One possible entry to this tale is through the last letter of the alphabet, Z. Abdias Nascimento ends his 'ABC of Quilombismo' in his seminal paper 'Quilombismo: An Afro-Brazilian Political Alternative' with '(z) Zumbi: founder of Quilombismo. Zumbi: zenith of this historical hour, zenith of this Black Afro-Brazilian people.'[3]

2 Sylvia Wynter, 'Black Metamorphosis: New Natives in a New World' (unpublished manuscript).

3 Nascimento, 'Quilombismo: An Afro-Brazilian Political Alternative', 168.

And indeed, there is no other figure that embodies the histories, the philosophies, the governance structures, the resistances, and the imaginations of quilombismo more than Zumbi. Zumbi dos Palmares.

The legend of Zumbi dos Palmares (c. 1655–November 20, 1695), the Brazilian *quilombo* leader of Kongolese origin who fought against the Portuguese in Brazil, who liberated Africans from the bondages of enslavement, who freed enslaved peoples from the plantations, who cultivated a society built not on oppression but on egalitarianism, who established systems of governance that can't be described in any way other than essentially democratic, who conceived a spirit of radical cultural emancipation—is one to be told over and over again.

The letter Z and Zumbi leads us to the work of the percussionist and vocalist Naná Vasconcelos. Born in Recife in 1944, the state of Pernambuco was the centre of Vasconcelos's life, just as it was for Zumbi. Vasconcelos was known for his mastery of a wide array of Brazilian percussion instruments, as well as the *berimbau*, a wooden bowed instrument. But it is the use of his body—as a musical instrument, as a transmitter of knowledge, as a site of potential—that is so compelling when it comes to this story.

When Vasconcelos released the album *Zumbi* in 1983, he already had legendary albums such as *Africadeus* and *Amazonas* (both from 1973) and *Saudades* (1979) under his belt. These releases all tackled aspects of Afro-Brazilian, African, and African diasporic histories and presents in some form. With the album *Zumbi*, he invoked one of the most powerful episodes of Afro-Brazilian—and world—history. And he chose his body as the narrator of that history.

On *Zumbi*, Vasconcelos seems to be activating the memory of his body, their bodies, our bodies, while simultaneously advocating for his body, their bodies, our bodies to *be* that site of transcendent discourse. In performing the music, he transformed his whole body into the skin of a drum, into a power source that could generate vibrations: the generative body. His limbs, abdomen, diaphragm, and ribs all became oscillators for sound. With every instance of clapping, stamping, biting, beating, tapping, whistling, and singing, Vasconcelos asked his body to speak—to speak of, from, by, through, with Zumbi. Zumbi dos Palmares. King of the Quilombos.

It is the story of Zumbi that Vasconcelos tells on his album of the same name, tangentially, metaphorically, somatically. In listening, one can imagine the scene in 1678 as Pedro Almeida, the Portuguese governor of the captaincy of Pernambuco, tries to convince Ganga Zumba, Zumbi's uncle and at that time King of Palmares, a group of runaway enslaved people who established community settlements, to accept a freedom deal. The deal would bring about (a form of) peace, but at the cost of placing Palmares under Portuguese authority. Listening further, one can also imagine Zumbi opposing his uncle and instead advocating for the freeing of *all* enslaved people and for total autonomy. Through the music, one can imagine Zumbi ultimately killing Ganga Zumba in 1678 and taking over the kingship. It is said that as King of Palmares, Zumbi set up economic, political, and cultural infrastructure that drew upon his Kongolese origins. A human-compatible alternative to the inhumanity and sheer barbarism of the plantations—a key reference for quilombismo.

Another possible entry to the tale is through Nanny of the Maroons, the eighteenth-century leader of the Windward Maroons, who were enslaved in the British colony of Jamaica. Nanny the Queen. Granny Nanny. Nanny, like Zumbi, celebrated in song—this time by Sons of Kemet on the track 'My Queen Is Nanny Of The Maroons' from their 2018 album *Your Queen Is A Reptile*. The sounding of the nyabinghi drums in the beginning of the track is an invocation of the spirit of Nanny. But the Sons of Kemet's horns also tell stories of resistance and emancipation that connect the African continent to its diaspora, as much as it connects all emancipation struggles around the world. Through the beatings of the goatskin bass baandu, the middle-pitched fundeh, and the high-pitched kete drums, Nanny the Queen makes her presence felt though another spirit being, Muhumuza (meaning the one who brings peace). Queen Muhumuza, who was possessed by the spirit of Nyabinghi (meaning abundance) in what is today Rwanda/Uganda/Tanzania, was fundamental in resisting the colonial occupations and violences bestowed upon her people.

The Sons of Kemet's pounding horn blows are reminiscent of the *abeng* cow horn used by the Windward Maroons and Nanny as they strategized, ambushed, and stood their ground against the British in the First Maroon War. As well as being revered for the ecstatic qualities of its sound, the abeng served as a long-distance communication device. Using this pre-telephonic technology, the Maroons could easily inform each other about the positions and conditions of the supposedly more sophisticatedly equipped British army. But the sound of the abeng was not the only technology the British were ignorant of in this battle. Just as Nyabinghi used the elements of earth, wind, fire, and water to win the war against the colonialists, so too did Nanny employ the supernatural technologies of her ancestors, the powers of *obeah*, to lead her people with zeal. Allying with the other eastern Maroons, Nanny and the Windward Maroons used guerrilla warfare against the British troops, stopping them from breaching the Blue Mountains, where the maroons had set up communities. Alongside Nanny were others, such as

Quao, Cudjoe, and Accompong, who led the Maroons to a form of freedom and self-determination. Accepting defeat on the battlefield, the British offered a peace treaty that was signed on 20 April 1740 and which provided more freedoms to the Maroons, granting them the 500 acres of land that is today Moore Town (formerly known as New Nanny Town).[4]

But this story, the story of quilombismo, though it needs key figures through which it can be told, is not about Zumbi, Nanny, Nyabinghi, or the many unnamed others. Another way into this tale is to tell it as the history of the pursuit of justice and the carving out of spaces of emancipation. It can—and must—be told as the history of long fights to create crevices through which the historically disenfranchised can breathe. It can—and must—be told as the long history of remonstrations and revolts against dehumanization of the people of the world by the people of the world.

As Sylvia Wynter succinctly puts it in her reflections on maroonage in 'Black Metamorphosis', the story must also be told as a 'quest for a free space from where to wage the ongoing process of revolt against the cultural colonization'.[5] One of the particularities of Wynter's statement is processuality. Emancipation is a process. Maroonage is a process. Quilombismo is a process of the elasticity of revolt. Once a free space is obtained after a fight, the *real* struggle begins through the maintenance

4 Karla Lewis Gottlieb, *The Mother of Us All: A History of Queen Nanny, Leader of the Windward Jamaican Maroons* (Trenton: Africa World Press, 2000), 95.

5 Wynter, 'Black Metamorphosis' (unpublished manuscript).

of that space—not only vis-à-vis the former perpetrators of violence but also the complacency of those currently in possession of power. In short, spaces of freedom and freedom itself must be continuously cultivated.

Nascimento expatiates on the fundamentals of the quilombo as a space of reunion, but even more importantly, as a philosophy and praxis of 'encounter, solidarity, living together, existential communion'.[6] This is at the core of quilombismo. Nascimento advances his delocalization of quilombismo as a non-spatial concept—or at least one that cannot be reduced to particular spaces—by thinking of quilombismo as a project of economic egalitarianism with the ultimate goal of achieving sociopolitical and human progress. It is important to reflect upon the fact that quilombismo was birthed during a period of existential violence perpetrated by the conceptualization of capitalism. This took place during a time when the world was conjured up by European colonialists to be made up of those working in plantations and those profiting from the wealth of those plantations. It is therefore crucial to consider quilombismo as an economic system, built on the 'adaptation of African traditions of communitarianism and/or Ujamaa' and an economic alternative that doesn't see work as a 'form of punishment, oppression or exploitation; work is first a form of human liberation, which the citizen enjoys as a right and a social obligation'.[7] Nascimento situates the essence and process of quilombismo as something that

6 Nascimento, 'Quilombismo', 161.

7 Nascimento, 'Quilombismo', 161.

is embodied and emanates from the tensions of struggle, repression, and resistance, which are still prevalent today—through the residues of the colonial enterprise, as debris of the capitalist Babel we have built in the last 600 years, as remnants of technologies of disenfranchisement and dehumanization. It is in such historical and present realities that quilombismo manifests itself as a philosophy of resistance through joy, as a space of practice of the technologies of enchantment, as real and facultative spaces of bliss and elation conceived around ethical and egalitarian values.

Another possible entry into the tale is through the multiplicity of spaces in which quilombismo has historically manifested and continues to exist. Through these spaces and their philosophies comes the revelation that humanity can unlearn the toxic concept of the human as *homo egocentricus* or *homo economicus* and relearn a concept of humanity and way of being in the world that is grounded in mutual respect, ethical values, and a shared dignity. This tale is about the big and small quilombos, cumbes, palenques, cimarrones, and maroons across the globe where the cultural, political, social, and economic tasks of liberation and emancipation are being imagined and exercised. As Nascimento points out, the quilombo phenomenon spread far and wide, taking different forms in different places. Even within Brazil, there were numerous manifestations of quilombos. As sociologist and anthropologist Roger

Bastide points out in 'The Other Quilombos', Palmares was the most famous and largest of all quilombos, but there were many others in Brazil whose histories attest to the 'collective flight and of resistance both to slavery and to the assimilation of white culture (as does its geography—many places are still named Quilombo, in memory of the Negro fugitives who settled there)'.[8]

Essentially, wherever there has been oppression, people have organized resistances of varying kinds. That is why the legends of fugitives who became maroons (*negres marrons*)—like Bazil in Guadeloupe; Linval or Les Alukus of Guyane; Anchaing, Cimendef, Roi Diamparé, Roi Mafati, Roi Phaonce, or Roi Tsymandevo in the Reunion Islands; Barbe blanche, Diamamouve, Madame Françoise, or Sans Souci in the Mauritius Islands; Makandal in Haiti; or Bayano in Panama—are and remain household names, still synonymous with defiance and liberation.

Another possible entry to the tale is to imagine a project titled *O Quilombismo: Of Resisting and Insisting. Of Flight as Fight. Of Other Democratic Egalitarian Political Philosophies* at Haus der Kulturen der Welt (HKW), Berlin, that brings together artists, scholars, activists, storytellers, and many others to deliberate on notions of quilombismo as historical facts, as spaces of fabulation and the imaginary, as contemporary realities, but also as metaphor. In the glossary at the beginning

8 Roger Bastide, 'The Other Quilombos', in *Maroon Societies: Rebel Slave Communities in the Americas*, ed. Richard Price (3rd ed., Baltimore: John Hopkins University Press, 1996), p. 191.

of Édouard Glissant's *Poetics of Relation*, we learn that the term maroonage originally described the political act of the fugitive, enslaved in Martinique, who escaped into the forested hills. Glissant describes how it has since come to designate:

> a form of cultural opposition to European-American culture. This resistance takes its strength from a combination of geographical connectedness (essential to survival in the jungle and absent in the descendants of slaves—alienated from the land that could never be theirs), memory (retained in oral forms and Vodou ritual), and all the canny detours, diversions, and ruses required to deflect the repeated attempts to recuperate this cultural subversion.[9]

O Quilombismo is an invitation to accompany and dwell in these psychic and physical spaces of the detour—to embody the discontinuity of narratives, to delve into the ravines and the back of the mountains, to explore the physical and metaphorical spaces of the camouflage, of disguise, and of fugitivity, past and present.

This invitation imagines what cultural resistance of our contemporary condition(s) could be, and how this might be informed by the cultural resistances and emancipation schemes of the past. In western thought, flight is often deemed to be a weakness, a failure. But in quilombismo,

9 Édouard Glissant, *Poetics of Relation*, trans. Betsy Wing (Ann Arbor: University of Michigan Press, 1997), xxii–xxiii.

flight is fight, flight as a precursor of fight, and flight as fight, giving the maroon the possibility of convergence, recalibration, and attack through guerrilla warfare.

This tale without beginning or end is staged as the first exhibition for a new era at HKW, accompanied by a series of discursive, filmic, and performative formats wherein sisterhood/brotherhood and free reunions, encounters of and for solidarity, and exercises of living together and practising existential communion are conceptualized and manifested; wherein those imaginations of sociopolitical and human progress in terms of the economic egalitarianism imminent in quilombismo are ruminated on and performed; wherein other ways of being in the world, like Ujamaa, form the basis of politics and economic systems are reflected upon; wherein that quest for a free space from where to wage the ongoing process of revolt against cultural colonization is visualized and materialized; and wherein a stage is set for a quilombist democratic egalitarian experience that factors in race, economics, sex, gender, society, religion, politics, justice, education, culture, and all expressions of life in society, and all levels of power within public and private institutions.

This is an invitation to quilombo—as a verb.

Bonaventure Soh Bejeng Ndikung

A Walk Through the *O Quilombismo* Exhibition

Quilombismo being an antiimperialist struggle, it articulates itself with Pan-Africanism and sustains a radical solidarity with all peoples of the world who struggle against exploitation, oppression and poverty, as well as inequalities motivated by race, color, religion or ideology.

—Abdias Nascimento, 'Quilombismo: An Afro-Brazilian Political Alternative'[1]

1 Abdias Nascimento, 'Quilombismo: An Afro-Brazilian Political Alternative', *Journal of Black Studies* 11/2 (December 1980), 155.

The exhibition *O Quilombismo: Of Resisting and Insisting. Of Flight as Fight. Of Other Democratic Egalitarian Political Philosophies* invites the public to engage with the artistic and intellectual threads marking historical and contemporary practices of cultural and political resistance and affirmation, while re-imagining Haus der Kulturen der Welt (HKW) as a more convivial, collective, and pluriversal house. *O Quilombismo* is composed of the rhythms of the aesthetic worlds it hosts, a vivid path that spans across different flows of art genealogies through and around the house.

Quilombismo philosophy, an anti-racist 'fraternal and free reunion, or encounter; solidarity, living together, existential communion'[2] leads us to open epistemological grounds to relate to a plurality of aesthetic lineages and knowledges that have resisted and insisted through (neo)colonization. The exhibition as a common space articulates quilombist 'radical solidarity'[3] by welcoming artworks and the worlds of Africa, the African diaspora, and communities from regions that resist oppression, both historically and in the contemporary. As a convivial space, *O Quilombismo* is driven by moves that loosen structures and hierarchies—physical, conceptual, and historical—asserting the agency of the many cultures and worlds in which people continue to live.

But what languages would such an exhibition speak? What forms can it summon and how would

2 Nascimento, 'Quilombismo', 161.

3 Nascimento, 'Quilombismo', 155.

they sit and move with each other? What spaces would it articulate? In the foyer, Tanka Fonta's mural follows an irregular serpentine surface in the modernist ensemble. Although rather narrow and easy to miss as an architectural element, its effect on the aesthetic and intellectual geometry of unity that the modernist building prides itself on is explosive. There is an immeasurable depth created by the cosmic background of the mural between the ceiling and the walls that is as consequential as the conceptual crack it evokes in an architecture that claims a single and coherent world, imagined by both the Cold War builders of this house and by their ideological opponents on the other side of the nearby Berlin Wall. Inside this surrounding gorge, echoes form, multiplying any single grammar of visual vocabularies into a polyphony of voices. Represented on the mural, there are movements of symbols, fables, alliances of resonance, traces of different Bamun scripts, recordings of sounds in different notation systems, visions of the forces in the universe and of quantic vibrations, science, and music. What all of these are not are abstractions; they do not exist in and for themselves, floating around a removed world that is unique and concrete, and they don't sit in any genealogies of abstract art. Nontsikelelo Mutiti's dazzling floor intervention in the Mrinalini Mukherjee Hall is not rooted in ahistorical abstraction either. This act is one of regrounding the foundations through the liberatory geometries of African braiding techniques and knowledge, alluding to the escape routes of people in the process of self-liberation and establishing *quilombos*, communicating necessary topographic information in secret throughout the community via braiding patterns. Further in the exhibition, Owusu-Ankomah constructs his works with adinkra signs as building blocks. A complex Akan system of signification and communication, adinkra signs are more than just letters and words. Concepts and stories are conjured by each sign, and their wisdom and imagination are inextricably bound to their form, while still extending largely beyond the formal. The free-standing walls in the exhibition compose together a *gyawu atiko*, an adinkra symbol that speaks about the courage to stand for and defend one's community. In the same key, Farid Belkahia (1934–2014) built his own artistic instruments by using visual references from Tuareg writing systems and forms used in healing and protection technologies. The textile makers Bastin Santan Diggekar, Shakirambi Ganishab Tattongi, Bibijan Babushab Gunjavathi, Hattarabi Maulasab Gunjavati, Badimabi Gafarsab Ugrani, and Saidambi Imamasab Naik of the Siddi Afro-Indian community found ways to speak at the same time about infinite worlds existing together on a single quilt by refocusing, repurposing, and giving life to materials that had previous lives. Marie-Claire Messouma Manlanbien crafts microcosms that fuse formal codes of Akan women's society with mathematical orders and popular culture.

The paintings by Abdias Nascimento (1914–2011), as well as the works of Rubem Valentim (1922–1991), are strongly based on the *orishas*, spirits of the Yoruba and Afro-diasporic religions, and are both crucial in reimagining artistic vocabularies within a Brazilian context and outside Eurocentric modernist genealogies. Foundational to Black world-making, Nascimento and Valentim both rely on Yoruban spirituality and on the figures of the orishas to organize their lives and artistic universes in ways that make realities vibrate and present to the viewer, irrespective of the forms found on the canvas. Against western modernism's 'exercise of pure abstraction', which Nascimento contested as 'an of "art for art's sake"',[4] abstract aesthetic trajectories of the exhibition are not reduced to form as they connect to historical and spiritual dimensions, troubling the binary of abstraction and figuration. In their near vicinity, Everald Brown (1917–2003) creates his own geometry of the cosmos, in his case, deeply rooted in Ethiopian revivalist beliefs. And it is this drinking from the springs of different spiritual systems that opens up another chapter in *O Quilombismo*.

Nascimento's great diversity of visual modes are represented in the exhibition as the project's symbolic architecture departs to an extent from his artistic world, as well as from his immediate Brazilian milieu with its vast multigenerational histories of contesting racism and crafting Afro-diasporic cosmologies with their own aesthetics as a form of politics and collective celebration. Alongside his geometric works, often based on devotional devices of the spirits, in *Oshunmaré Rising* (1972), there is a more vivid representation of the spirit of the rainbow. The painting is also an inspiration for the colour palette used on the different walls, floor, and seating throughout

4 Abdias Nascimento, 'Afro-Brazilian Art: a Liberating Spirit' in *Abdias Nascimento – Being an Event of Love*, eds. Amal Alhaag, Aude Christel Mgba, Bonaventure Soh Bejeng Ndikung, Gwen Parry, Ibrahim Cissé, Krista Jantowski, Zippora Elders (Berlin: Archive Books, 2022), 73.

the exhibition. Brown's works are also multilingual, including images of Haile Selassie as the Rastafarian God and his musical instruments. This inclusion of multiple religious and spiritual references in the exhibition is an acknowledgement of the different cosmological systems that have always coexisted. Artistic languages as well as technological imaginations are each derived from specific cosmologies. This is present throughout key points in the exhibition, from its very beginning in Tiergarten, on the flagpoles lined up along the alley approaching the entrance, and with the blessings and welcoming in of the works by María Magdalena Campos-Pons, dedicated to the different orishas.

The exhibition then moves to the works of Alberto Pitta, based on his practice of adorning floats and designing entire processions during Carnival celebrations across Brazil, and displayed here as two murals on the facade, celebrating Ogun, the orisha and Yoruba deity of Candomblé known for his path-opening powers as well as metallurgy and technology in general. The artists of Taller Portobelo hail from a maroon community of African descent from Panama, the *cimarron* of Portobelo. Through their work, they craft a visual culture (Arte Congo) around the traditions of art, dance, Carnival, and other technologies of joy making and sharing, keeping alive an ever-growing and evolving spiritual pantheon. Gwladys Gambie recreates an Afro-Caribbean deity, insisting on the sovereignty of ancestral spiritualities. Eustáquio Neves, incorporating a profound knowledge of contemporary Afro-Brazilian religious practices into his work, offers an invocation rooted in Candomblé. Through the care of memory and accountability, Charmaine Watkiss creates drawings of warrior female figures that remind us of the power of plants in the African diaspora, while Ana Beatriz Almeida invokes the West African spiritual figure of the *griot*—a community storyteller. In the same vein are the artworks that constitute part of Carnival's culture of self-affirmation, such as in the works by Demond Melancon of the Young Seminole Hunters.

Beyond the Atlantic geography, Li Jiun-Yang imagines a fantasy world born from the distinctive Taiwanese spiritual folklore of the past centuries, unruly and self-organized outside and against the claims of Chinese imperial rule. Rotimi Fani-Kayode (1955–1989) draws from West African pre-colonial understandings of gender and sexuality and deities to craft their dissident identity and their relationship to HIV/AIDS in the early years of the pandemic in the eighties. Quilombist philosophy is thus also understood in the exhibition as a process of liberating one's self, abolishing the constraints of gender, and of other forms of body normativity. This is also in dialogue with the history evoked by the Magnus Hirschfeld Bar at HKW, which is on the precise location where the Institut für Sexualwissenschaft (Institute for Sexology) was founded in 1919 before being destroyed by the National Socialists. Alongside Fani-Kayode's work, queering plays an emancipatory role in Joshua Serafin's work, exploring analogous roots from their native home country of the Philippines, but with four decades of queer revolution in between him and Fani-Kayode.

The interest in the body—both individual and collective—as a shrine of resistance, constitutes another major thread throughout the exhibition. The power of women's energy shines through Hayv Kahraman's large-scale paintings, creating another level of representation in the Sylvia Wynter Foyer, one that embraces the viewer and animates that point of entry into the exhibition. Diana Ejaita's work populates a large wall connecting in-between spaces, illustrating bodies as bridges to a spiritual world from West African narratives. Lizette Nin's work narrates a related story, where the seeds needed for establishing a new economy of quilombos would be hidden in hair. Lisa Hilli employs references to fashion to research the crucial role played by women in the anti-colonial political and cultural movements of Melanesia, which saw some of Asia Pacific's most radical projects for re-establishing societies independent from any parameters derived from the colonizers. In the same line of approaching fashion from a feminist and anti-racist perspective, and with a strong presence in that world, Carol Barreto brings the strength of women from contemporary quilombos through the materiality of textile making. Bruno Zhu departs from the realm of clothing as a device to obscure and reveal, crafting his own quasi-totemic figure not unlike Fani-Kayode or Serafin, but composed from an entirely contemporarily derived queer mythology.

At the core of the quilombist project has been the affirmation and celebration of life, the possibility of existence in dignity, and the joy of being able to take this for granted. At the heart of *O Quilombismo*, forming a kind of nucleus that celebrates this, is a digital presentation of works from the Museu de Arte Negra (founded by the Teatro Experimental do Negro and Nascimento in 1950), which illustrates the insistence of the exhibition's subtitle through an unencumbered Black quotidian. Works by Maria Auxiliadora extend this, with a focus on gardening and the generative force of making the soil fertile on one's own terms. Kaylene Whiskey imagines women's worlds of joyous resistance from her Yankunytjatjara country, in what is now known as Australia, through global pop culture icons. Mallica 'Kapo' Reynolds (1911–1989) brings to life a moment of play in the forest of Jamaica, while Laeïla Adjovi brings in testimonies from contemporary quilombos.

Quilombismo philosophy opens further epistemological grounds for museum propositions that lead us to pluriversal practices, which de-universalize models of experiencing and preserving culture, uncovering ways to repair inequality and engage with culture as a living activity. From the aforementioned Museu de Arte Negra, whose mission was to contest racism and the invisibility of Afro-Brazilian culture in museums, to the contemporary initiative *El Museo Afroviviente* by the collective Hermosa Intervención, founded in 2020 by Afro-Uruguayan women to perform the histories of significant Afro-diasporic women who have been overshadowed from historiography, artists like these make interventions into stagnant museum structures and make way for possibilities to transform and transcend their experiential limits. Other works and practices engage a similar endeavour: Assaf Gruber destabilizes museums' hidden works in their repositories, while acts of cultural revitalization by Tuli Mekondjo and Glicéria Tupinambá recreate works displaced by colonial museums as restitution to their communities, the Aawambo people in Namibia and the Tupinambá community in Serra do Padeiro in Bahia, respectively. In the same vein of thinking, the exhibition presents efforts to imagine differently how functions of historiography and care could be practised outside of the colonial legacy of museums.

The exhibition is thus multigenerationally constructed and includes key historical pieces that map several intellectual and political genealogies that have imagined and affirmed Black power in the Americas, each having been reflected in visual universes and references. Alongside aforementioned artists, Albert Artwell (1942–2018) marks a key moment in the rich generations of cultural life and struggle in Jamaica from the movement around Marcus Garvey to the Rastafarian and Ethiopian revival religious movements, each having promoted and centred Black liberation and African legacies in opposition to British colonial rule. Within this debate and aesthetic quest that has straddled decades, grounded in newly crafted spiritual horizons woven through their works, Artwell evokes pan-Africanist transatlantic connections of the twentieth century and the era of independence struggles, in dialogue with another Nascimento work, made in solidarity with the fight for freedom of the Angolan people. Jasmine Thomas-Girvan's contemporary perspective on another historical strand of Black history departing from the work of Fitz Balintine Pettersburg adds to this landscape.

The quilombos on which Nascimento based his thinking have always been plural political formations, where ways of living together, shared spiritual horizons, and aesthetic parameters have been negotiated between people of different backgrounds, hailing from various places on the African continent, from Black communities already rooted in the Americas, persecuted communities in Europe, such as Jewish refugees from the Iberic Peninsula, as well as individuals from various Indigenous nations in the Americas, dislocated by colonizers. In tracing the multiple legacies of the quilombist experience, the exhibition is also working with artists from various backgrounds who reclaim an Indigenous perspective. Bernardo Oyarzún reconnects with ancestral Mapuche mythology; Nikau Hindin revives the Māori practice and technology of bark cloth making in Aotearoa/New Zealand; and Celia Vasquez Yui summons a parliament of more-than-humans as seen through a Shipibo visual lens—a work that also resonates with Truong Cong Tung's canvas roll, sculpted by a colony of termites.

The generative political power of the quilombist principle continues to inform contemporary political debates and struggles. In the exhibition, Olu Oguibe challenges us to reconsider the fundamental issues of our times by placing them at the highest level of symbolic political discourse, on the flagpoles on HKW's terrace, facing the nation's highest institutions of power, organized in an urbanistic choreography of pomp and circumstance. Elsewhere, Ange Dakouo weaves large textiles made of newspapers that also embody the protective amulets of the Donso community in Mali. Artist and activist Zica Pires establishes continuities from a younger generation and as a form of renewal of the affirmative power of art in the political struggles for sovereignty that her community—the quilombo Santa Rosa dos Pretos—faces. Sawangwongse Yawnghwe explores the political, economic, and cultural entanglements in Myanmar's Shan State and more broadly in the mountainous area of continental South East Asia with a history of eluding state control, while focusing on the recent uprising in Myanmar following military takeover. Resonating through several corridors in the building, Anand Patwardhan presents a poem-song of resistance in the struggle against casteism in the Indian context, an ever-urgent political issue in the country.

By creating spaces of hospitality and performativity, the exhibition is also part of an effort to reimagine HKW and to propose a new politics of welcoming. Artists have thus been invited to intervene and reconfigure spaces inside and outside the building, often altering and appropriating spaces of rigidity or of impersonal transit. Georgina Maxim embellishes the columns at the entrance, transforming—along with Alberto Pitta's exuberant mural—the grey and anonymous modernist symmetry of the facade into a sensorial and storytelling path to receive the audience. Transitioning into the central foyer, which is simultaneously recreated as a social space and oasis of respite, Amina Agueznay intervenes with henna-dyed weavings of wool and metal strings on the foyer's larger columns. The same space is further resignified through the living forum of political affirmation in the work of Barby Asante. Lastly, Temitayo Ogunbiyi's work in one of the reclaimed exterior spaces of the institution convenes a common space outdoors, interlinking a seating area with sound for the citizenry and living beings that surround the Spree River.

Cosmin Costinaș and Paz Guevara

Artists and Works in the Exhibition

Anna Seghers & Semra Ertan Gardens

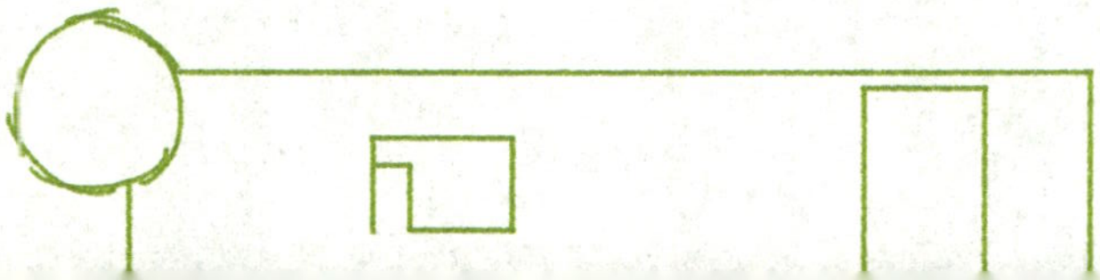

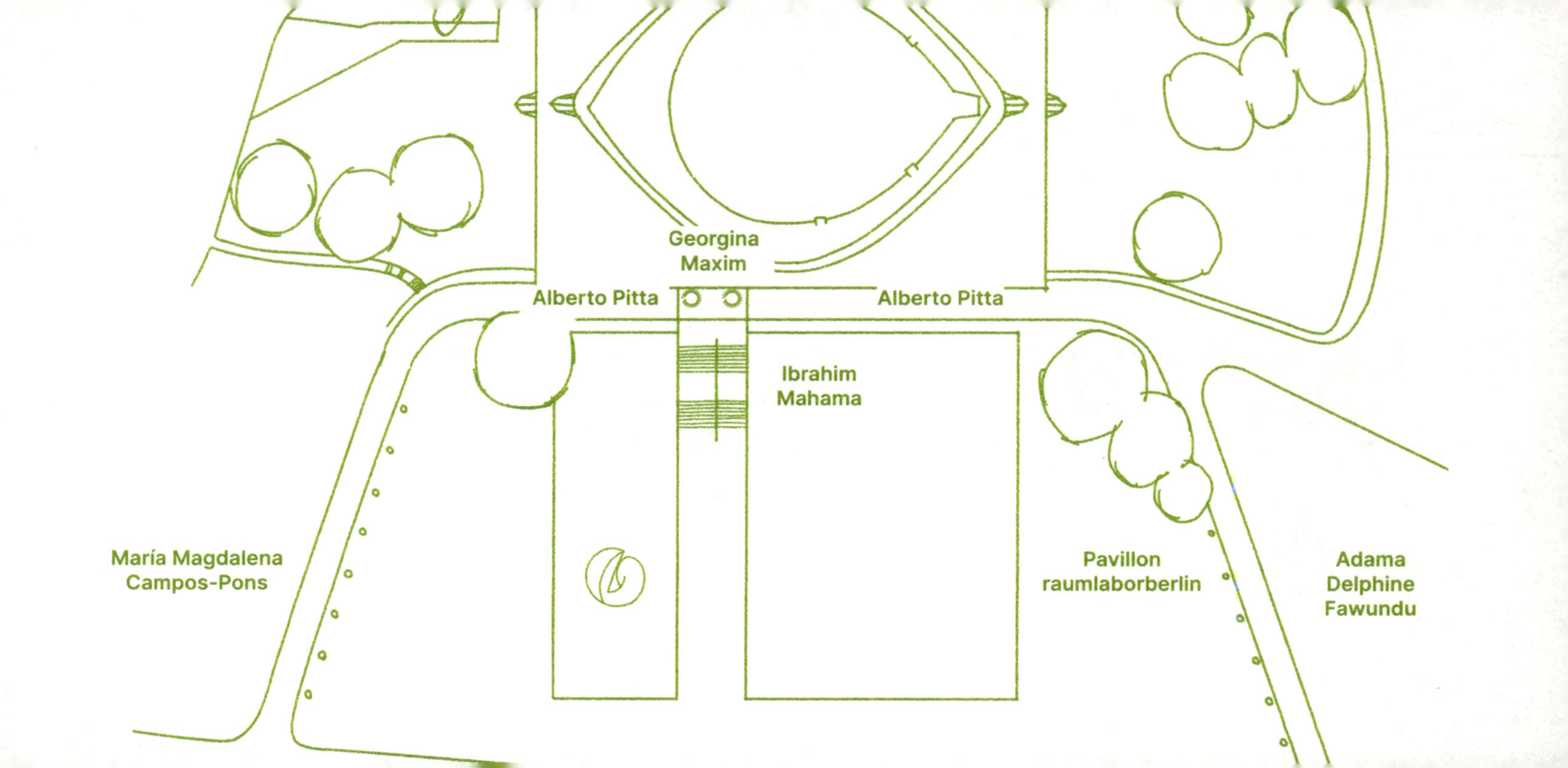

Georgina Maxim
Alberto Pitta
Alberto Pitta
Ibrahim Mahama
María Magdalena Campos-Pons
Pavillon raumlaborberlin
Adama Delphine Fawundu

María
Magdalena
Campos-Pons

Adama
Delphine
Fawundu

Ibrahim Mahama

1959, Matanzas, Cuba,
lives in Nashville, US

María Magdalena Campos-Pons

Throughout her artistic practice María Magdalena Campos-Pons connects worlds. By acknowledging her Yoruba and Chinese roots in a Cuban context, Campos-Pons has created a large body of work that affirms Afro-Cuban and diasporic cultures, stressing the complex layers of history that societies can embody. She recollects stories and knowledges passed on by her family as well as through archives, intertwining the personal and intergenerational with the historical. Her work often opens a dialogue with the generations of Africans who, like her ancestors, worked on sugar cane plantations in Cuba and resisted enslavement through spiritual and cultural practices such as Santería, the Afro-Cuban religion where Yoruba beliefs have been kept alive. The artist's generous method of shaping a 'felt history' offers compassion and understanding amidst these fractured times. For HKW's main entrance, Campos-Pons has created a series of flags that flutter with the vibrant symbols of Yoruba *orishas*, spirits that welcome visitors with their blessings. Commencing with the flag of Oshun, the river orisha related to femininity, fertility, beauty, and love, the flags are a gesture of hospitality, an invitation to connect with the colour codes emblematic of the orishas' spiritual protection, and co-celebrate worlds of conviviality, healing, tolerance, respect, and joy. —PG

Commissioned by Haus der Kulturen der Welt (HKW), co-produced by María Magdalena Campos-Pons and HKW, 2023.

When We Gather, Performance by María Magdalena Campos-Pons, Baba Murah & Ensemble, Forum Brasil and Ilê Obá Sileké, Candomblé House in Berlin, and Rasiel Almanza Cairo on Friday, 2 June, 16:30, see p. 259.

Detail. Courtesy of the artist

Work in the exhibition:
Prayer Flags (2023), installation of eight flags, prints on fabric, 235 × 150 cm each
Courtesy of the artist

Detail

Adama Delphine Fawundu

1971, Brooklyn, New York City, US, lives there

Adama Delphine Fawundu can trace her family history several generations back to Equatorial Guinea and to Mano, a small island off the coast of Sierra Leone. The signature blue colour in her work is a reference to water and the various streams that are witnesses to many ages. She considers water to be the element that connects living beings to the universe but also to histories and stories of human life across geographies. With the installation of sixteen newly commissioned flags at the entrance of HKW, Fawundu's work draws a poetic connection to the history of the former congress hall, its creation, and positionality. She sees these flags as 'dancing with our ancestors and earth/universe energies to make way for our future'. The aesthetics of her work weave together recurring West African traditional symbols and materials to highlight a rootedness in knowledges that hold answers to contemporary struggles and help oppose narratives of hierarchy and oppression. —MHP

Commissioned by Haus der Kulturen der Welt (HKW), co-produced by Adama Delphine Fawundu and HKW, 2023.

Work in the exhibition:
***When the Spirits Dance* (2023), sixteen flags on eight poles, prints on textile materials, 100 × 260 cm each**
Courtesy of the artist

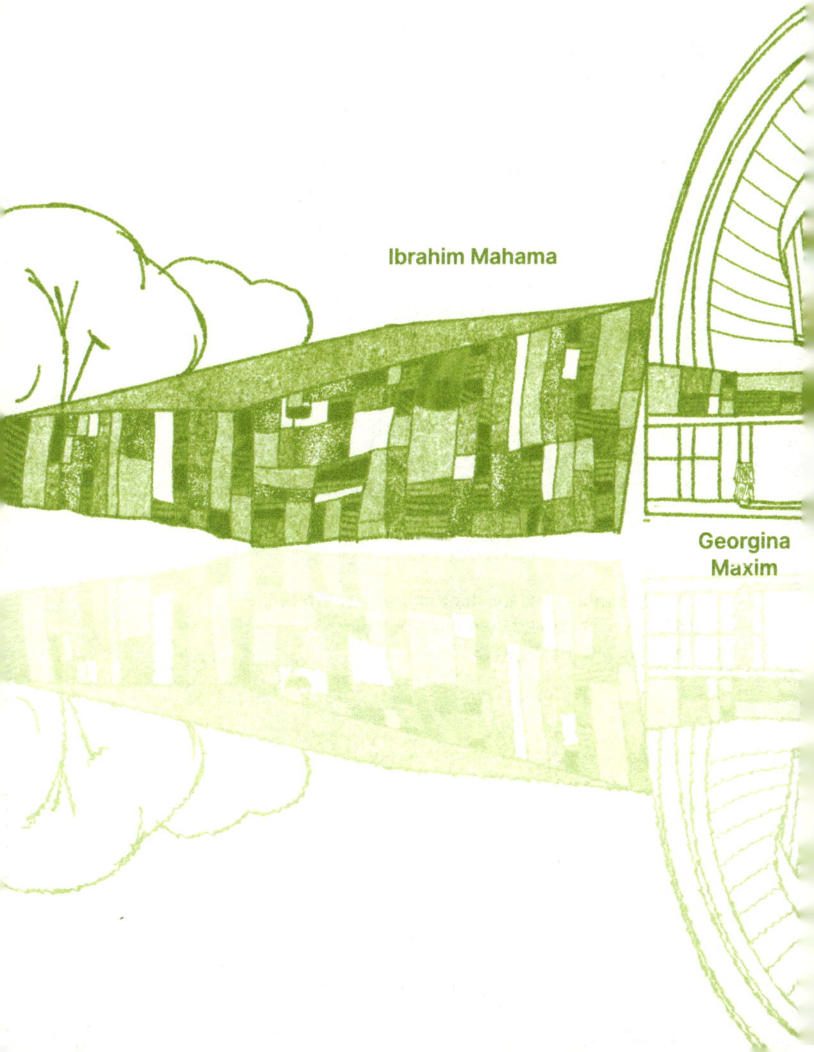
Ibrahim Mahama
Georgina
Maxim

Alberto Pitta

Work in progress. Photos: Jeferson Lima

1961, Salvador de
Bahia, Brazil, lives there

Alberto Pitta

Since the late 1970s, Alberto Pitta has been creating textiles that affirm and celebrate Afro-diasporic culture in Brazil. Created using a silk-screen printing technique, Pitta's exuberant fabrics have contributed to the Afro-Bahian aesthetic that brings Carnival to life, incorporating embroidery motifs, spiritual symbols of the diasporic Candomblé religion, and documentary photography. His textiles often honour Afro-Bahian cultural practitioners, such as the artist and Candomblé priest Mestre Didi. From his studio in Bahia, Pitta designs the outfits and entire processions of the Afro blocks, the Afro-Bahian carnival associations that parade through the city avenues during the celebration. Pitta's practice lies in the 'stories that textiles can tell'—a medium to rescue, preserve, transmit, and enliven cultures, while also a means of self-affirmation and liberation against racism. For *O Quilombismo*, Pitta has created a series of canvases transforming the facade into a passage of visual storytelling. One side of the mural welcomes visitors into the world of Ogum, a Yoruba deity of Candomblé known for his path-opening qualities, who is celebrated by quilombist, anti-colonial communities to this day. The other side shows the communal housing of contemporary *quilombos* in Bahia standing with pride, announcing the stories to come of a HKW that re-opens as a Haus of many houses. —PG

Commissioned by Haus der Kulturen der Welt (HKW),
co-produced by Alberto Pitta and HKW, 2023.

Works in the exhibition:
Ogum que são sete [Ogum who are seven] (2023);
Moradismo: estéticas de quilombo [Moradismo: aesthetics of the quilombo] (2023), mural, 2 series of serigraphy on canvas, fourteen serigraphies, 345 × 300 cm each. Courtesy of the artist

Works in progress. Photos: Tatenda Gora

1980 in Harare, Zimbabwe,
lives there

Georgina Maxim

Growing up in newly independent Zimbabwe, artist and storyteller Georgina Maxim has developed an artistic practice that centres the revival of memory and collective writings of untold stories. First as a way of finding and strengthening the lifeline that connects her to her deceased mother, and then as a tool to connect threads of histories from the past to the future. By stitching together textiles from Zimbabwe, mixed with personal clothes she collects from people, she creates tapestries that stand as witnesses of time, but also constitute a metaphor for the ephemerality of life and the fragile presence of human beings on earth. The practices of stitching and weaving found in traditions from the African continent and across the world are often associated with the making of symbolic garments used in rituals of initiation or to mark significant transitions such as birth, marriage, or death. Care, patience, and resilience are required for the hands that connect memory together through such practice. As a contribution to the physical environment of HKW and the collective memories brought into the space through *O Quilombismo*, Maxim drapes two of the columns in the main entrance with her majestic tapestries—and by extension the care, love, and resilience embedded within them. —MHP

Commissioned by Haus der Kulturen der Welt (HKW), co-produced by Georgina Maxime and HKW, 2023.

Works in the exhibition:
Borrowed books and underlined statements I (2023), textile, 325 × 270 cm; *Borrowed books and underlined statements II* (2023), textile, 214 × 315 cm. Courtesy of the artist

1987, Tamale, Ghana,
lives there

Ibrahim Mahama

For the past decade, Ibrahim Mahama has been interested in objects in a state of decay, transforming them to explore themes of migration, globalization, and economic exchange in relation to the history of Ghana. His large-scale installations employ materials gathered from urban environments, junkyards, or abandoned buildings. These can include remnants of wood, metal, or jute sacks, but also historical textiles that transmit previously silenced memories and stories. In realizing *E PAIN ME* as well as *IN THE GARDEN*, the two sculptural tapestries he puts in conversation with HKW's historic architecture, Mahama employs stitching techniques inspired by traditional weaving practices widely found across West Africa. In creating these canvases of memory, he poetically engages in a healing process while unearthing and translating their embedded knowledges to a contemporary audience. From the junkyard owners who collect objects in decay to the weavers the artist invites as co-makers, collaboration is essential to the realization of the work. Mahama places a strong importance on passing down skills and memory through artistic creation, aiming to shift paradigms of education and knowledge circulation while also performing collective acts of rewriting history. —MHP

Commissioned by Haus der Kulturen der Welt (HKW), co-produced by Ibrahim Mahama; Red Clay Studio, Tamale; and HKW, 2023.

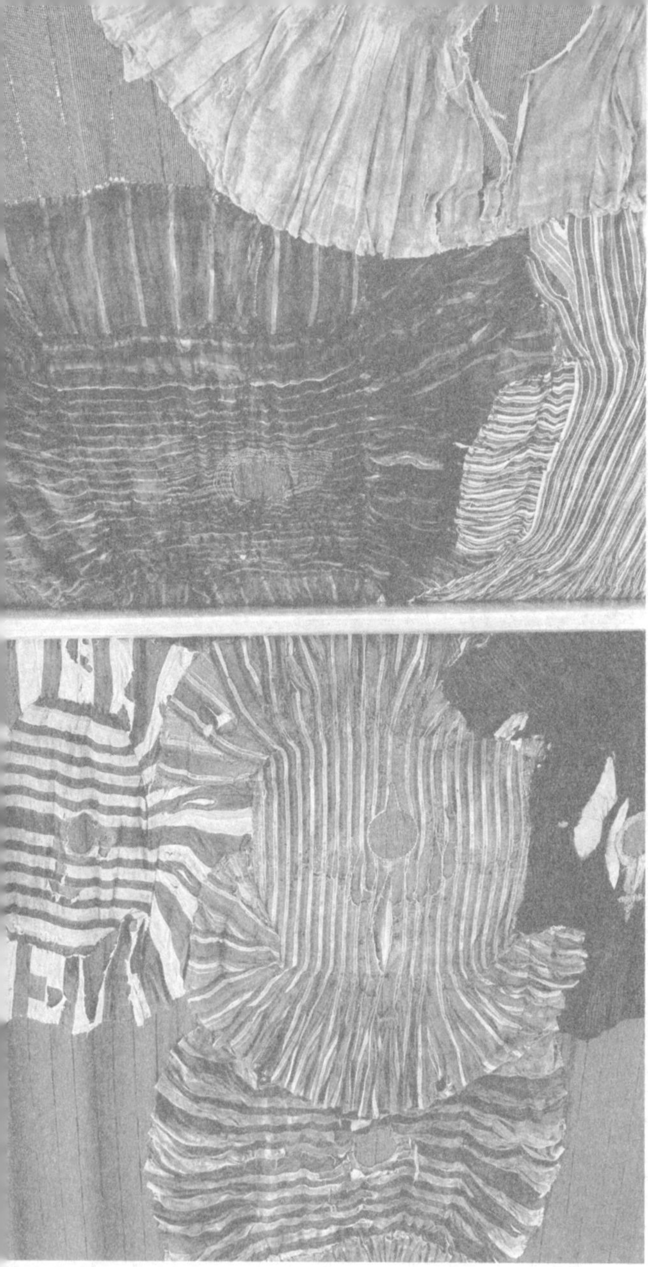

E PAIN ME. Photos: the artist

Works in the exhibition:
E PAIN ME (2023), installation of historical hand-woven fabrics, synthetic cotton, 20 × 30 m (Les Nana Benz Terrace); *IN THE GARDEN* (2023), installation of historical hand-woven fabrics, synthetic cotton, 19,6 × 4,5 × 19,1 × 9,1 m (Anna Seghers and Semra Ertan Gardens). Courtesy of the artist; Apalazzo Gallery, Brescia; White Cube Gallery, London, Hong Kong, New York, Paris, West Palm Beach; and Red Clay Studio, Tamale

Sylvia Wynter Foyer

Tanka Fonta

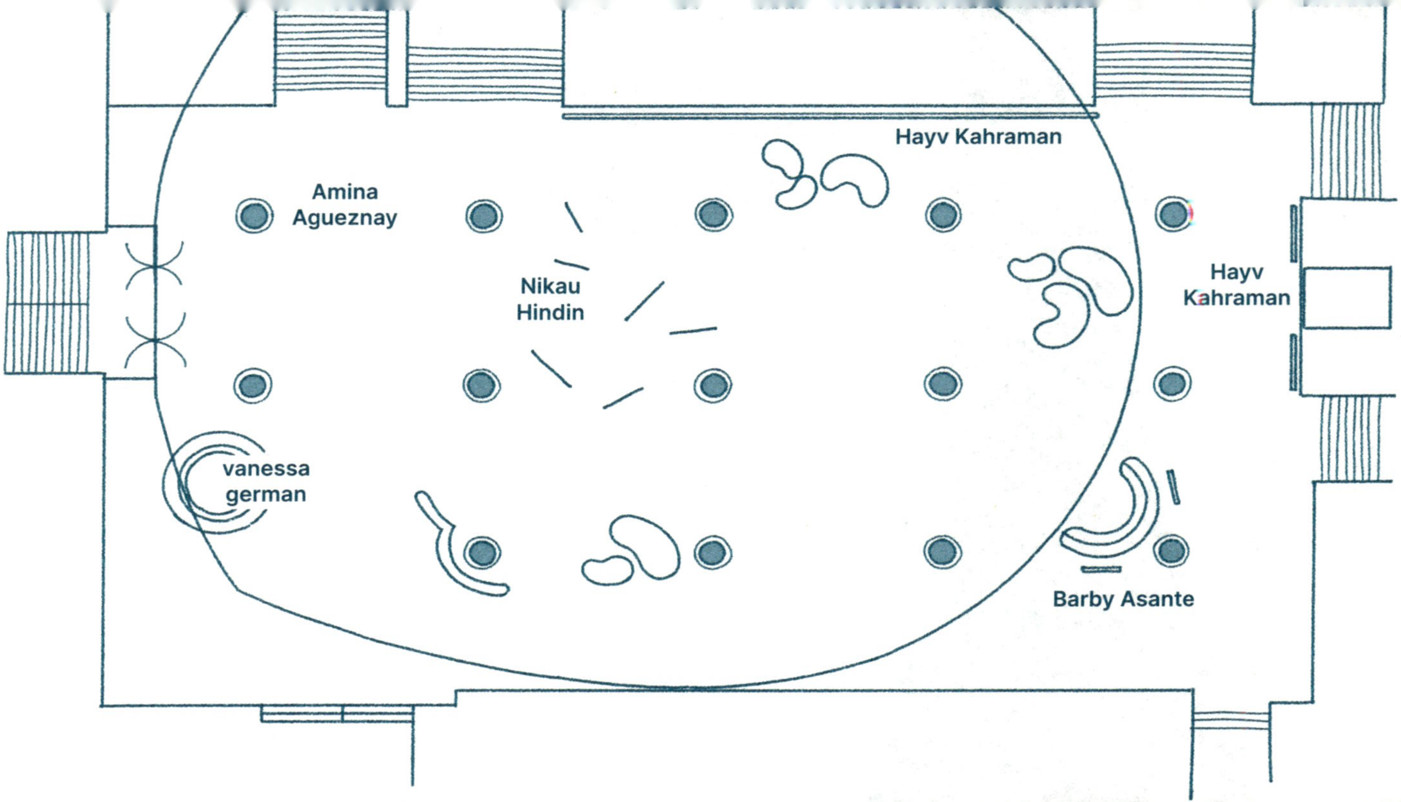
Hayv Kahraman
Amina
Agueznay
Nikau
Hindin
Hayv
Kahraman
vanessa
german
Barby Asante

Tanka Fonta
Amina Agueznay
vanessa german at reception

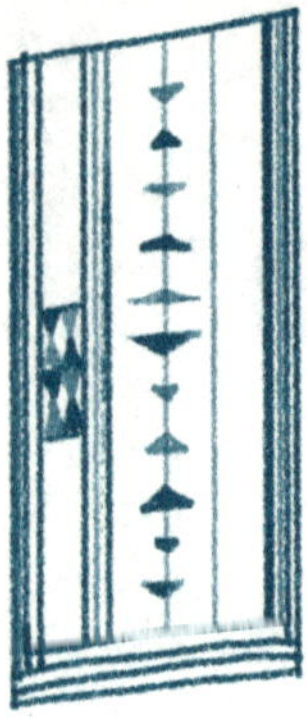

Nikau Hindin

1966, in Buea, Cameroon,
lives in Berlin, Germany

Tanka Fonta

Tanka Fonta is a composer, artist, author, performer, instrumentalist, poet, researcher, and scholar of African music. Fluent in diverse musical idioms and genres, he often integrates themes and motifs from different musical cultures of the world—a strong and converging point in his works and compositional palette that he describes as the following: 'The emerging mural work in HKW is a picto-sonic composition of nine thematic movements, orchestrated in evocative symbolic languages as visual, sonic, and poetic imprints. It integrates and aggregates the non-verbal languages of different fields of intuitiveness, receptivity, non-visual awareness, and sensitivity, considering the visible or non-visible phenomena outside the ranges of one's analytical thoughts and learned languages. We are inviting, proposing, and asking the perceiver to participate, explore, and enter into the immersive language of evocative mysteries and the murmurs of the cosmos. The mural is artistic storytelling in visual and sonic form, integrating alternative non-western philosophical inquiries from deep time, as well as the collective stories of a shared humanity and its journeys and experiences'.

To fully experience the work, an orchestrated anthem will be performed in order to lead the visitors' auditory senses through Fonta's visual journey. —MHP/TF

Commissioned by Haus der Kulturen der Welt (HKW), co-produced by Tanka Fonta and HKW, 2023.

Sound performance by Tanka Fonta with Eden Meier and Saliou Cissokho on Saturday, 3 June, 15:00, see p. 264.

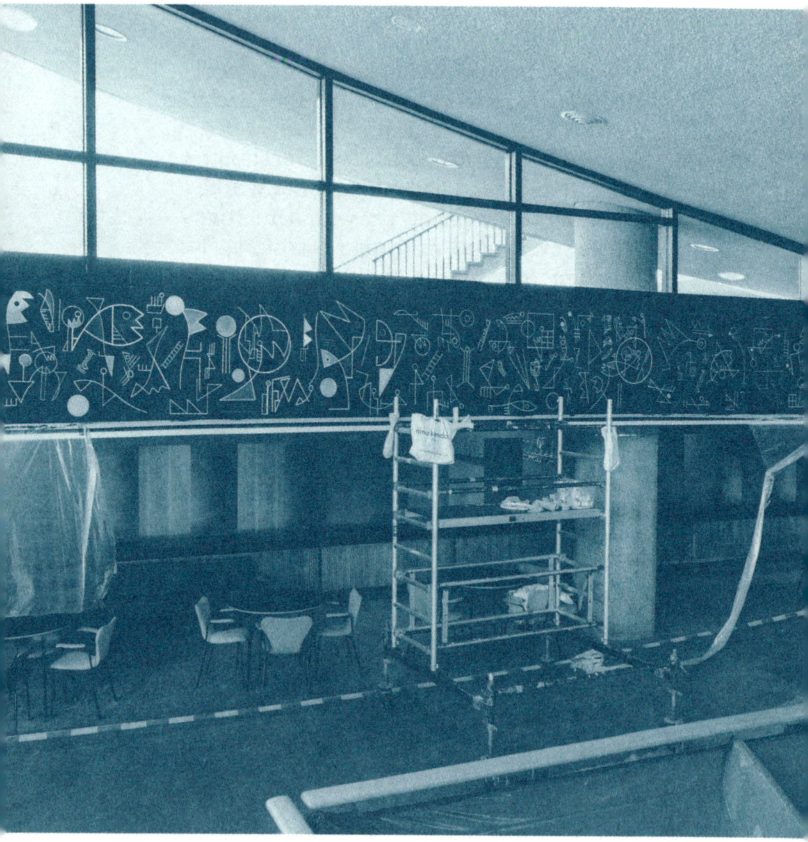

Detail, Sylvia Wynter Foyer. Photo: Alexander Steffens/HKW

Work in the exhibition:
The Cosmogenic Interconnectedness 'How Did We Talk Before the Roman Alphabet?' The Picto-Sonic Dialogues I, mural (2023), dimensions vary, comprised of 9 elements: *The Cosmogenic Interconnectedness 'How Did We Talk Before the Roman Alphabet?' The Picto-Sonic Dialogues I*; *Epistemic Interrelatedness I: 'I Have Eaten of the Sun II'*; *To This Earth We All Belong: 'Di Kontri Meeting II'*; *There Never Was a Beginning Nor an Ending*; *Dictionary of Non-Time, Time Transcoders & Transformers*; *Vibrations of Memory & Deep Time: 'The Meditative Movements of Perception & Understanding'*; *The Thought Transformers I: Do I Need to Look Like You to Be Considered a Living Being*; *Has the Stream Flowed?*; *The Dawn Incantations I*. Courtesy of the artist

1963, Casablanca, Morocco,
lives in Marrakesh, Morocco

Amina Agueznay

Before dedicating herself to an artistic practice, Amina Agueznay worked as a full-time architect while also learning the craft of jewellery design. Asserting that everybody has 'a connection to handicraft and handmade things', her work allowed her to engage deeply with her native Morocco, even while studying or working elsewhere. Agueznay often explores her country's immaterial cultural heritage, directing numerous workshops with weavers, carpenters, leatherworkers, basket weavers, and masters of other handicrafts. Her artistic projects are joint undertakings with teams of craftspeople, working together from conception to realization. The works often play with size, volume, and materiality, incorporating influences that oscillate between the fields of architecture and jewellery design, respectively. For her site-specific commission as part of *O Quilombismo*, Agueznay transforms several columns in the foyer into an oasis of respite and sociality, covering six of them in a special material woven from wool yarn spun on metal wire. The airy work also has the quality of a fungus growing from a tree trunk, breaking the symmetry of the modernist lines that otherwise define the space. The henna with which the wool is dyed is a key element with a rich history as a pigment that also has protective and auspicious qualities —a propitious start for this opening exhibition and the new direction of HKW. —EFB/CC

Commissioned by Haus der Kulturen der Welt (HKW), co-produced by Amina Agueznay and HKW, 2023.

Work in the exhibition:
Assetta #2 (2023), natural undyed and naturally dyed wool yarn, metal wire, cotton thread, glue, dimensions vary
Courtesy of the artist

Assetta (2016), installation view, Société Générale Atrium, Casablanca, 2016. Photo: Guy Thimel. Courtesy of Société Générale

1991, Ngāpuhi, Te Rarawa, Tāmaki Makaurau [Auckland], Aotearoa New Zealand, lives in Turanganui a Kiwa [Gisborne], Aotearoa New Zealand

Nikau Hindin

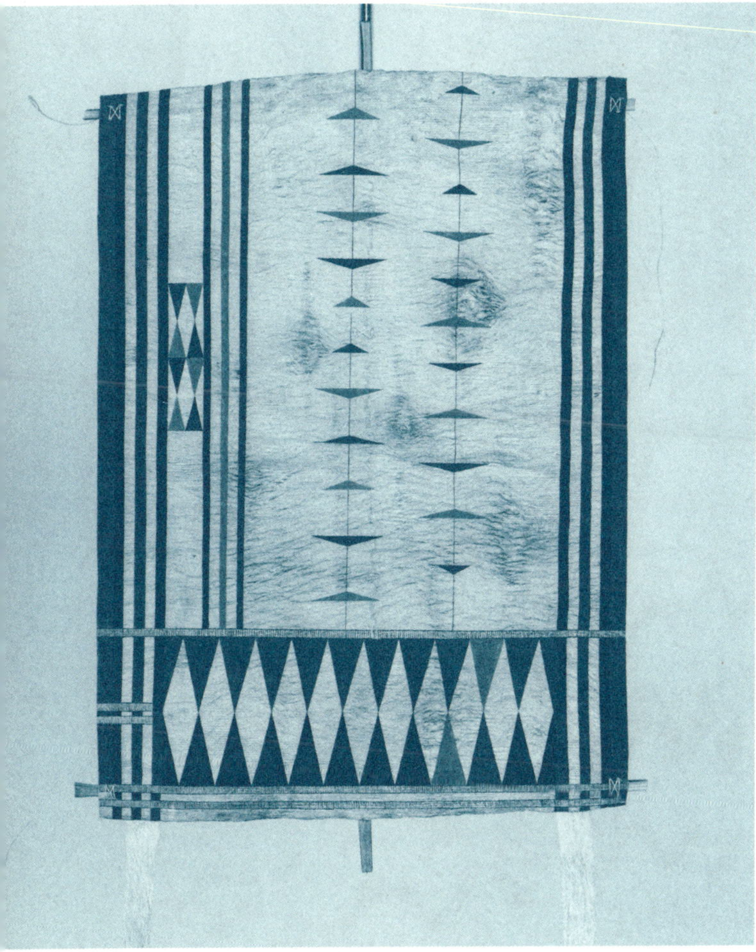

Detail. Photo: Seb Charles

Work in the exhibition:
Manu Aute: Rere Runga Rawa: Ascend to the Higher Realms (2022–23), kites, mixed natural materials: *kōkōwai* (earth pigments) on *aute* (paper mulberry bark cloth) with supplejack and raupo frames and *muka* (flax) cordage with *tikumu* (mountain daisy), dimensions vary. Courtesy of the artist

Detail. Photo: Holly Burgess

Nikau Hindin is a contemporary Māori artist deeply engaged in the renewal of the Māori *aute* (bark cloth) making tradition in Aotearoa/New Zealand. Bark cloth is a major cultural language in the Pacific, an art form and technology which spread together with the migration of the Austronesian ancestors of the Māori and of other nations in the Pacific (and Indian Ocean), who likely carried the mulberry trees from their original homeland in Taiwan throughout the Pacific for this precise purpose. Unlike other Pacific bark lineages, the Māori bark cloth technique that Hindin employs was last practised in Aotearoa more than a century ago when, under the impact of colonial exploitation of land and resources, the paper mulberry tree that is the main source of bark was almost made extinct. While also including other motifs from Māori culture as well as other designs, architecture, and textile traditions in the works shown, Hindin uses the bark as an instrument to express another Indigenous technological lineage, the kites or *manu*. Manu means both kite and bird in Māori, and while often used for recreation, they were also used for divination, communication, as well as a guide to new auspicious lands to settle on. —CC

Commissioned by Haus der Kulturen der Welt (HKW), co-produced by Nikau Hindin and HKW, and realized with the support of Creative New Zealand, 2023.

1976, Milwaukee, US,
lives in the US

vanessa german

The practice of vanessa german, who identifies as a citizen-artist, is invested in the possibility of connecting with each other, one person and one moment at a time. The modes in which she works traverse sculpture, performance, installation, community activism, and collective rituals. With *RELEASE: a living ritual for letting go* she offers viewers an invitation—literally embedded with seeds and the potential of flowering. Take this card, and go on an intentional stroll around HKW. In german's cosmos, healing and making a new start might be as simple as taking the first steps toward something, without an exact destination. In this 'intimate pilgrimage', visitors—in solitary contemplation or brought together in the context of the exhibition—are invited to consider the traumas around us, of the earth, of this city, of the building that houses HKW, and of all the myriad experiences and histories that come together, and take a step towards releasing. What would happen if we would come together and walk hand in hand? With *Hand in Hand: a love poem for togetherness* german proposes this deceptively simple question, trusting all the possible outcomes of this humble yet most generous of touches: joy, discomfort, a sense of belonging, grace, shared breath, shared steps, dirt under our feet. —JW/A

Commissioned by Haus der Kulturen der Welt (HKW), co-produced by vanessa german and HKW, 2023.

RELEASE: a living ritual for letting go **and** ***Hand in Hand: a love poem for togetherness*** **by vanessa german at the opening, see pp. 257 & 263.**

Works in the exhibition:
RELEASE: a living ritual for letting go **(2023), participatory performance / score, text printed on paper pulped with flower seeds;** ***Hand in Hand: a love poem for togetherness*** **(2023), participatory walk / collaborative performance**
Courtesy of the artist

Blue Walk, The Union for Contemporary Art, 2019
Courtesy of The Union for Contemporary Art

Blue Walk, The Frick, Pittsburgh, PA, 2021
Photo: Heather Mull

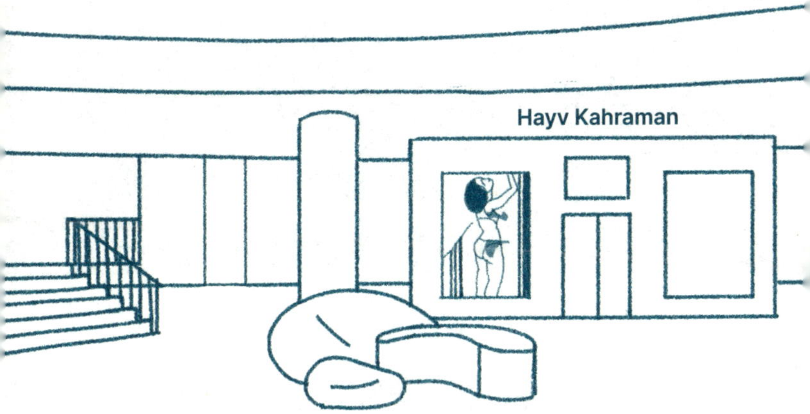
Hayv Kahraman

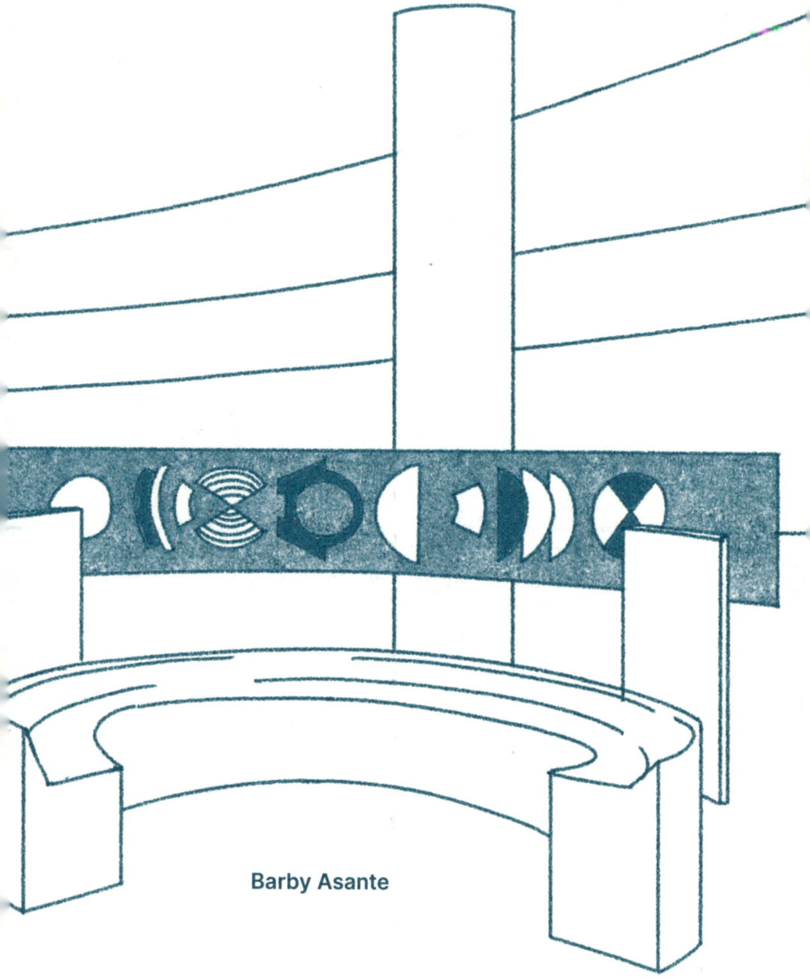

Barby Asante

1971, London, UK,
lives there

Barby Asante

In her artistic practice, Barby Asante focuses on everyday methods and strategies of decolonization to discuss the ways in which historical and personal events are remembered, misremembered, or forgotten. In many of her works, concrete physical as well as affective spaces are created to interrogate the politics of memory by examining the effects of political structures on mnemonic processes. By inviting others to contribute, Asante emphasizes her conception of an integral, collaborative, performative, and dialogic practice. The ongoing work *Declaration of Independence* recreates a physical space reminiscent of congressional chambers, where treaties of independence, trade deals, manifestos, and legislative policies are produced, negotiated, and approved. In this performative re-enactment, the forum-like space is inhabited by women of colour who engage actively as 'contributor-collaborators'. Together they form a chorus sharing different personal narratives related to the legacies of slavery and colonialism as a response to Ama Ata Aidoo's 1992 poem 'As Always a Painful Declaration of Independence'. The voices come together in video installations, sound pieces, and live performances centring the role of women of colour in world history as a collective act of learning and healing. —AOW

Courtesy of BALTIC Centre of Contemporary Arts, Gateshead.

A live performance of *Declaration of Independence* takes place on 12 August. For further information visit www.hkw.de.

Declaration of Independence, exhibition views, BALTIC Centre for Contemporary Art, Gateshead, 2019. Photos: Colin Jones

Work in the exhibition:
Declaration of Independence (2017–ongoing), video installation, live performances, sound pieces, 52' 26"

1981, Baghdad, Iraq,
lives in Los Angeles, US

Hayv Kahraman

Hayv Kahraman is a multidisciplinary artist whose work examines identity, memory, gender, and exile. Drawing from her personal history, her work investigates agency and body politics in relation to the feminized body across paintings and sculptures, combining influences from Europe, Asia, and the Middle East. Rather than serve as self-portraits, Kahraman's figures represent manifestations of the collective experiences of women of colour in the wake of colonization. The depictions of these bodies deconstruct European ideals by challenging preconceptions through complex conceptual and narrative techniques. In these new works the figures are painted on linen that is treated using a marbling technique. The work is marked by an ambiguity that comfortably references traditional and modern patterns highlighting an interdependence among the figures. By using feminized figures to link the past and present, the artist gives voice to a collective consciousness that is expressed through the forms and narratives she employs. The result is a reflection on the body as both object and subject, exploring commodification, survival, confrontation, and healing. —DMV

Commissioned by Haus der Kulturen der Welt (HKW), co-produced by Hayv Kahraman and HKW, 2023.

Works in the exhibition:
Untitled **(2023), oil and acrylic on linen, 292.1 × 139.7 cm**
Untitled **(2023), oil and acrylic on linen, 292.1 × 139.7 cm**
Untitled **(2023), oil and acrylic on linen, 127 × 127 cm**
Untitled **(2023), oil and acrylic on linen, 127 × 182.9 cm**
Untitled **(2023), oil and acrylic on linen, 127 × 182.9 cm**
Untitled **(2023), oil and acrylic on linen, 243.8 × 127 cm**
Untitled **(2023), oil and acrylic on linen, 243.8 × 127 cm**
Untitled **(2023), oil and acrylic on linen, 243.8 × 127 cm**
Courtesy of the artist and Pilar Corrias, London; Jack Shainman Gallery, New York; and Vielmetter Los Angeles

Untitled **(2023), oil on linen, 292.1 × 139.7 cm. Courtesy of the artist; Pilar Corrias, London; Jack Shainman Gallery, New York; and Vielmetter Los Angeles. Photo: Jeff McLane**

Mrinalini Mukherjee Hall

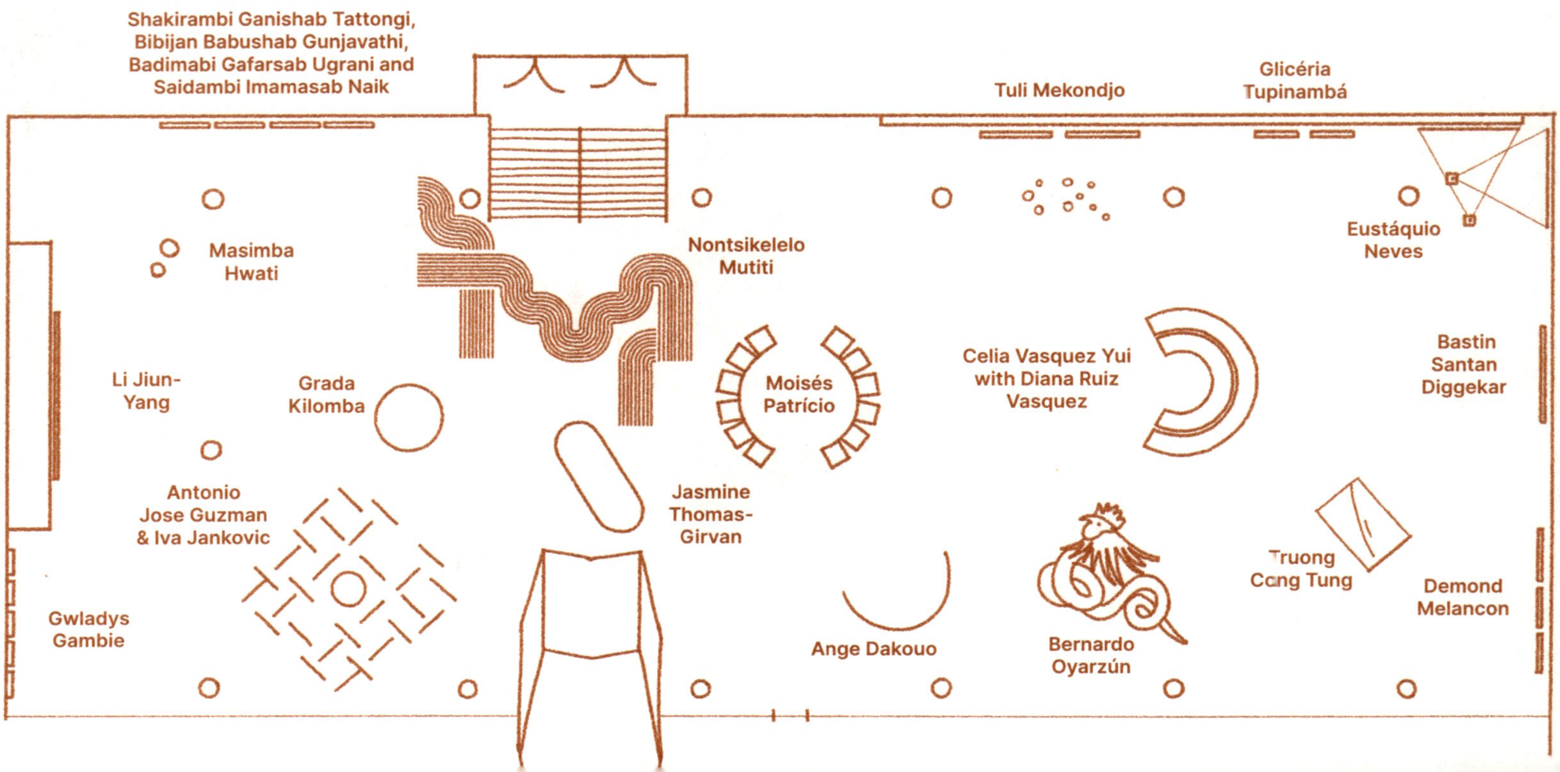
Shakirambi Ganishab Tattongi, Bibijan Babushab Gunjavathi, Badimabi Gafarsab Ugrani and Saidambi Imamasab Naik
Tuli Mekondjo
Glicéria Tupinambá
Masimba Hwati
Nontsikelelo Mutiti
Eustáquio Neves
Moisés Patrício
Celia Vasquez Yui with Diana Ruiz Vasquez
Bastin Santan Diggekar
Li Jiun-Yang
Grada Kilomba
Antonio Jose Guzman & Iva Jankovic
Jasmine Thomas-Girvan
Truong Cong Tung
Demond Melancon
Gwladys Gambie
Ange Dakouo
Bernardo Oyarzún

Ange Dakouo

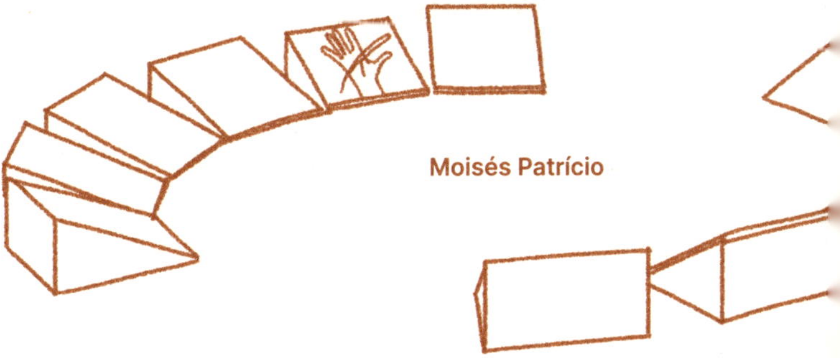

Moisés Patrício

Jasmine
Thomas-Girvan
Nontsikelelo
Mutiti

Artist's study for *Kubatana (togetherness / unity / connecting / touching / holding)*

Nontsikelelo Mutiti

For more than a decade, artist and designer Nontsikelelo Mutiti has been investigating and experimenting with the braiding of African hair as a technology of African culture rooted in specific aesthetics and knowledge. An ancestral medium to express social roles and group belonging, braiding was also repurposed to design hidden maps to escape the bondages of slavery, weaving together strands of hair along political paths of emancipation. Within the Black Power movement of the 1960s, braiding became an emblem of African beauty, pride, and affirmation throughout the African diaspora as a language that resisted colonization and forced migration. Mutiti's works are composed through samples and repetition, engaging with the mathematical knowledge of braiding to create patterns and rhythms, like an act of algorithmic calculation. Inspired by hair braiding salons—as places of kinship, identity, and intergenerational knowledge transmission—Mutiti's work produces a public space in which people can connect. By intervening in the exhibition space through a floor mural, spreading the liberatory motives of braiding all along its path, her work regrounds the foundations of the space, animating each person to walk and decode, and to celebrate the dynamic life of braiding practices as a form of resistance and joy. —PG

Commissioned by Haus der Kulturen der Welt (HKW), co-produced by Nontsikelelo Mutiti and HKW, 2023.

Work in the exhibition:
***Kubatana (togetherness / unity / connecting / touching / holding)* (2023), floor mural, floor paint, laser cut stencils. Courtesy of the artist**

1984, São Paulo, Brazil,
lives there

Moisés Patrício

That the body is a site of discourse and a space for deliberation is not a mere metaphor for Moisés Patrício, an initiated Candomblé priest, who has literally made his own hand his primary artistic and spiritual medium and material. Since 2004, Patrício has been *reading* his palm, allowing his hand to activate other beings and objects as he invites them to find space in his hand, offering its contents and messages to humanity and the spirits. Despite the histories of disenfranchisement, dehumanization, and subjugation, African peoples around the world have tried to keep the spirit of offering alive, whether they be material or immaterial, such as 'the pact of joy' offering that Patrício's grandfather always spoke to him about. And as many of these ancestors have made clear, these offerings do not expect something in return—it is an offer to the universe. A gift that is not transactional like the colonial, extractivist, and capitalist models of giving that demand a multifold and disproportionate return, this series of photographs, *Aceita?*, asks the viewer, the beholder, the world, if they are ready to accept a non-transactional world system that embodies a generosity for generosity's sake, irrespective of profit. —BN

Work in the exhibition:
***Aceita?* [Do you accept?] (2013–ongoing), photo series, 50 × 50 cm. Courtesy of Estudio Ikoritá**

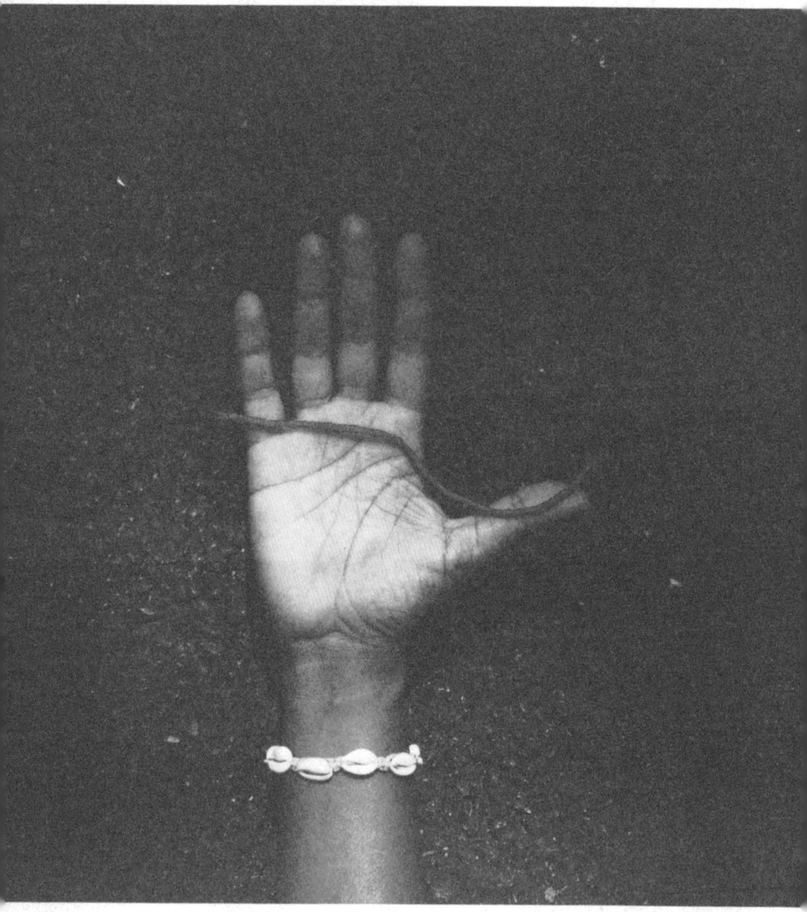

Detail

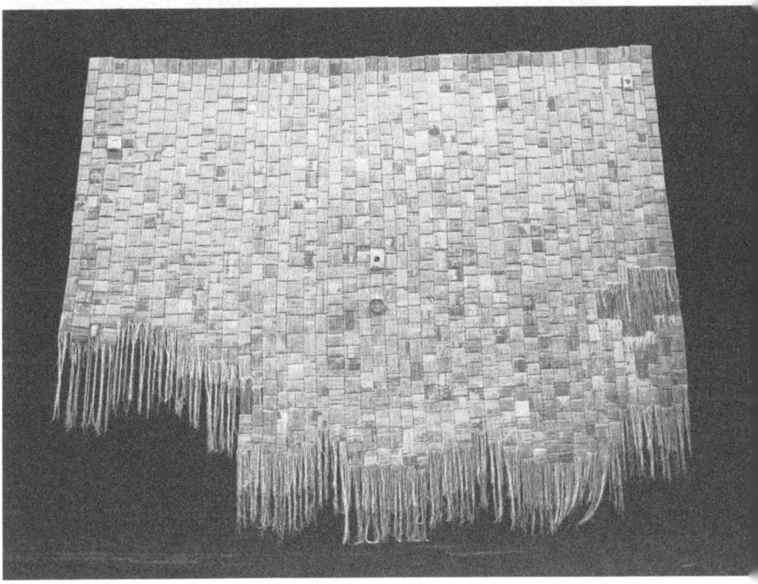

Photos: Salim Cissé

**1990, Abidjan, Ivory Coast,
lives in Bamako, Mali**

Ange Dakouo

Ange Dakouo was introduced to spiritual practices and rituals that centre the connection between human and non-human beings by the Donso community he originates from. The *talisman*, also known as a *gris-gris* or an *amulette*, constitutes a protection tool made from the wisdom of ancestral beliefs carried by living priests and priestesses who hold the responsibility of protecting the community. Throughout his artistic education and endeavour, Dakouo has reflected on how talismanic objects could be used to convey messages in the contemporary era, underscored by a fierce belief in their importance and protective power. Comprising a constellation of talismans held together by cotton yarn, the work presented by Dakouo constitutes a metaphorical representation of various societies and asserts the need for human threads to be woven together in order to thrive. The artist thus follows a long tradition of weaving practices that carry knowledge of communal living and solidarity that are commonplace in most African communities. —MHP

Commissioned by Haus der Kulturen der Welt (HKW), co-produced by Ange Dakouo and HKW, 2023.

Work in the exhibition:
Imagine **(2023), sculpture, cardboard, newspapers, cotton threads, leather, mirrors, iron, 275 × 350 cm**
Courtesy of the artist

1961, Kingston, Jamaica, lives
in Port of Spain, Trinidad

Jasmine Thomas-Girvan

Jasmine Thomas-Girvan is known for her aesthetic of assemblages which combine literary, oral, and performative practices with the visual. As Annalee Davis has stated, Thomas-Girvan 'binds varied materials together, connects the logical, linear plane with the supernatural, and links the human interior space with exterior realities.' *The Healing Stream* is an installation that unfolds like a scroll. Drawn on black paper, it centres Rastafari culture and pays homage to *The Royal Parchment Scroll of Black Supremacy* from 1926 by proto-Rastafarian preacher Fitz Balintine Pettersburg. The title *The Healing Stream* stems from a Jamaican folk song that urges: 'Dip dem in the healing stream/ Dip dem deep, but not too deep/ Dip dem to cure bad feelings', reminding the viewer that Black history engages with the power of healing through preached words, whether in song or in service. *The Promised Key*, on the other hand, is a small sculptural work that upholds the 1926 pamphlet under the same name published by Leonard Howell or the 'first Rastafarian' under his Hindu pen name G.G. Maragh. Preaching the history of redemption of Black people through space and time, Howell was later arrested for sedition and became a lifelong target of the colonial government for his activism. —AOW

Works in the exhibition:
The Healing Stream **(2022), installation, paper, graphite, acrylic, wood, L: 360 cm (Mrinalini Mukherjee Hall);** ***The Promised Key*** **(2023), 7.6 × 7.6 × 10.1 cm, installation, glass, sterling silver, paper (Beatriz Nascimento Hall);** ***Babylon's Fortune foretold...But what about us?*** **(2022), installation, transparent film, wood, 22.6 × 29 × 7.5 cm (Beatriz Nascimento Hall). Courtesy of the artist**

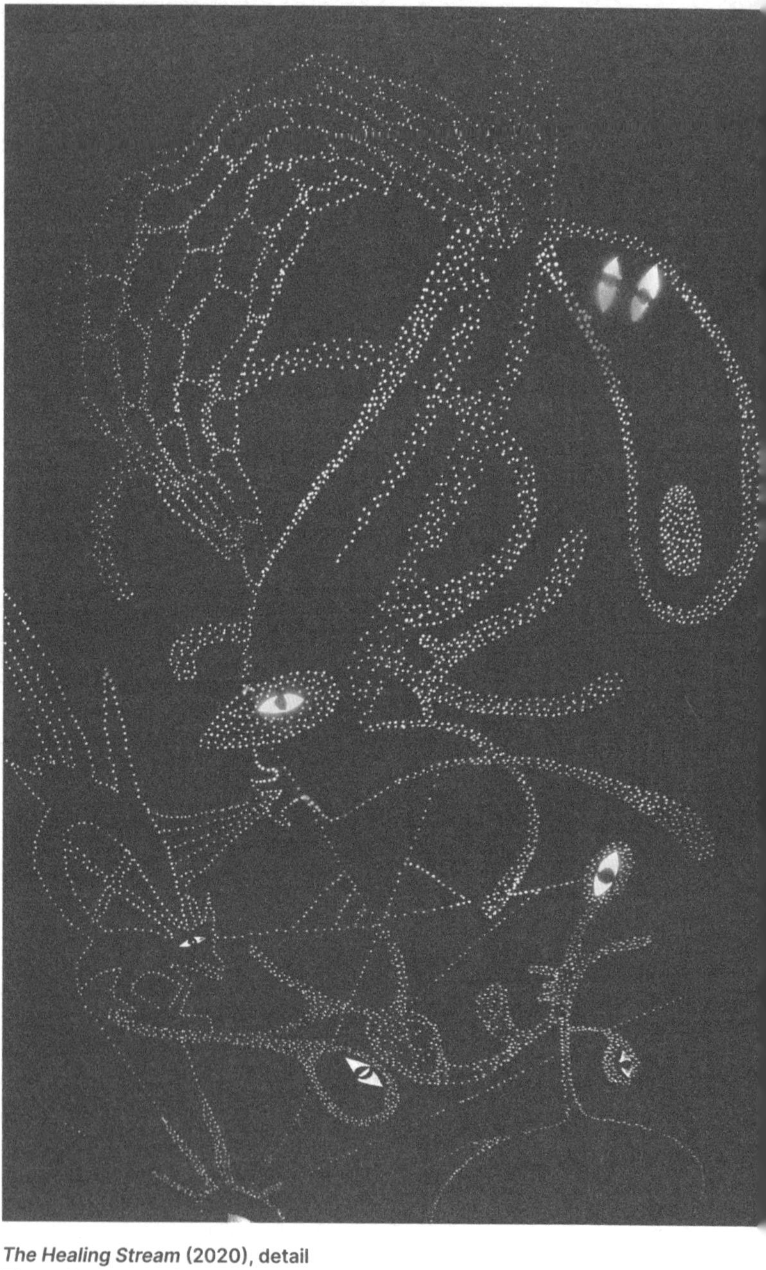

The Healing Stream (2020), detail
Photo: Nathan Patrick

Tuli Mekondjo

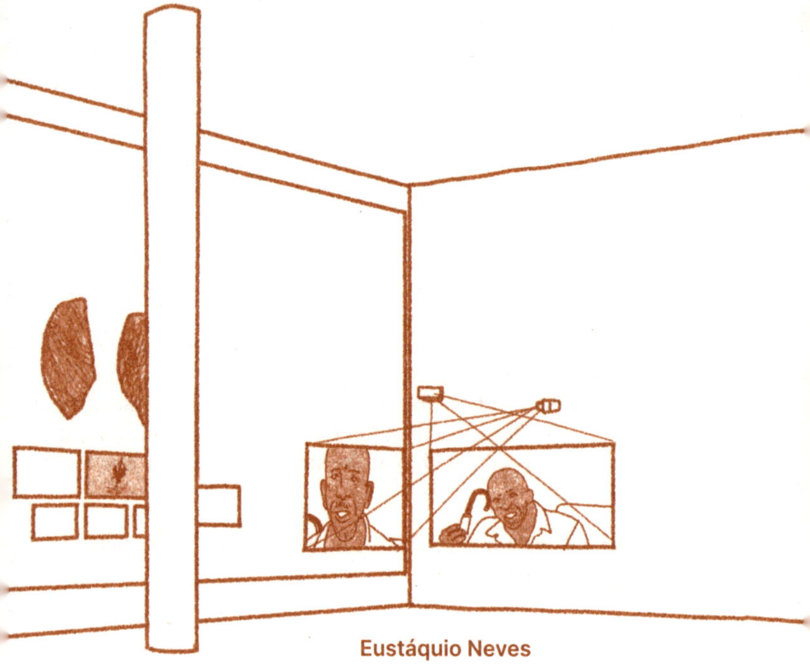

Eustáquio Neves

Glicéria Tupinambá

1982, Kwanza-Sul, Angola, lives in Berlin, Germany, and Windhoek, Namibia

Tuli Mekondjo

Born in exile during Namibia's war of independence (1966–89) and within the historical context of the trauma of the country's past under Germany's violent colonial rule (1884–1915), Tuli Mekondjo's artistic practice has been a labour of belonging, re-creation, and restitution. Her work is based on the stories she carries with her from her family and community in Namibia—where she returned after the country gained independence in 1990—as well as in her persistent research with and against colonial archives. In *Ounona vedu*, Mekondjo recreates a series of fertility dolls, which were formerly passed down from generation to generation to practise motherhood and connect to fertility in her community, the Aawambo people, while her canvases recompose a context through which archival photographic portraits of Aawambo women return the colonial gaze. By burning, washing, embroidering, cutting, and mending, the canvases become a space of transformation, to heal and honour the interrupted ancestral lineages. Her works draw the viewer into the renewing force of life that bonds and births generations. Mekondjo proposes a reimagining of restitution as the restoration of ancestral fertility channels and their strength to remember and recreate beyond institutional museum repatriation centred on ownership. —PG

Commissioned by Haus der Kulturen der Welt (HKW), co-produced by Tuli Mekondjo and HKW, 2023.

Works in the exhibition:
Ovadali vounona (Birthers of children) I **(2023), painting, silk fabrics, linen fabric, archival image transfer, cotton embroidery threads, paint markers, acrylic paint, gold leafing marker, copper leafing marker, 270 × 217 cm;** ***Ovadali vounona (Birthers of children) II*** **(2023), painting, silk fabrics, linen fabrics, archival image transfer, cotton embroidery threads, paint markers, acrylic paint, gold leafing marker, copper leafing marker, 270 × 217 cm;** ***Ounona vedu (Children of the soil)*** **(2023), installation, wood, antique glass beads, shell, shell beads, cowrie shells, copper beads, seeds, safety pins, human hair, nails, brass beads, suede, leather, springbok fur and skin, buttons, metal beads, ostrich egg shell beads, suede, cotton yarn, cotton fabric, linen fabric, rusted metal rings, sticks, red ochre, modelling clay, dimensions vary. Courtesy of the artist**

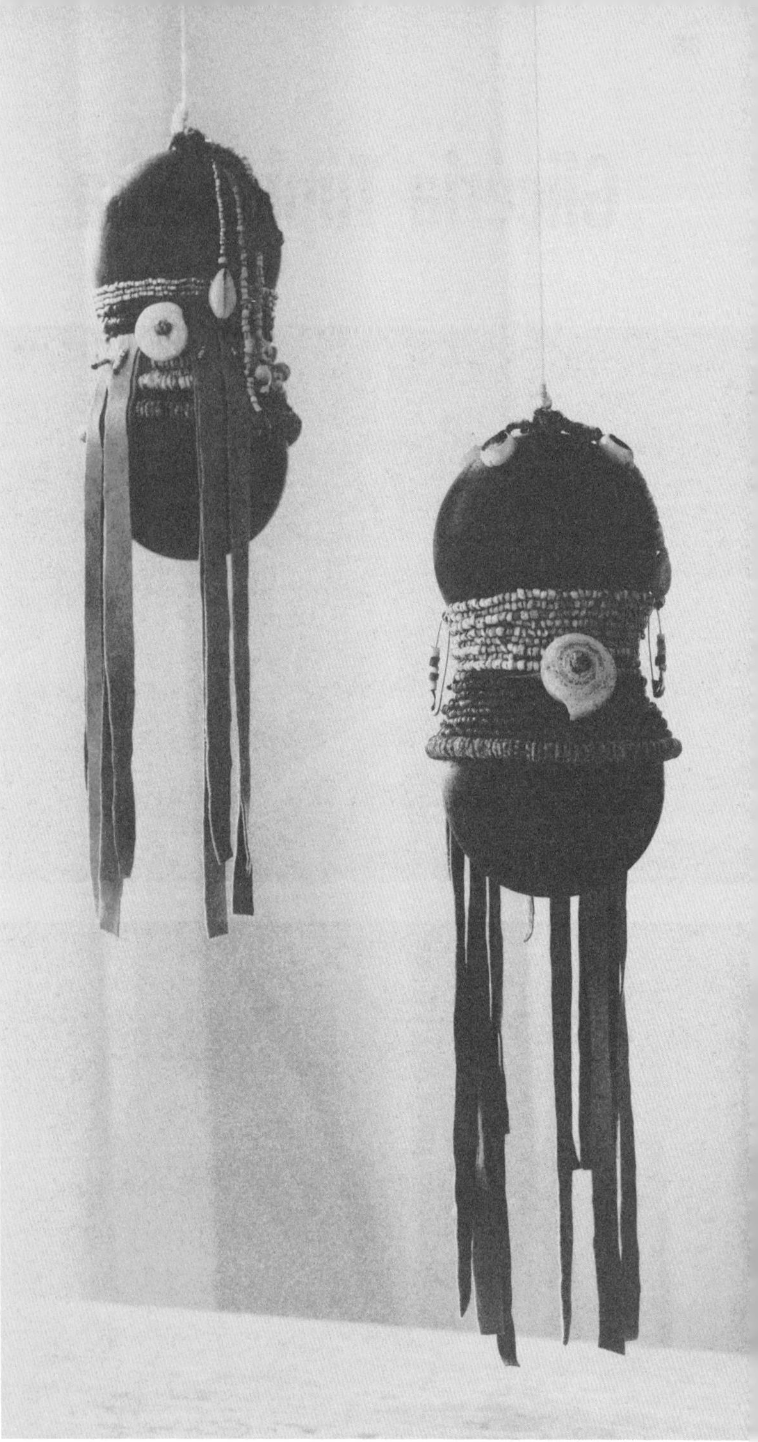

Ounona vedu (Children of the soil), detail
Photo: Jasper Kettner

Glicéria Tupinambá

Glicéria Tupinambá and Túlio Rosa, *Tupinambá Ybaka* (2023), video stills © Túlio Rosa

1982, Serra do Padeiro, Tupinambá Indigenous Land of Olivença, Atlantic forest in the south of Bahia, Brazil, lives in Serra de Padeiro

Active leader, Indigenous women's rights advocate, intercultural educator, intellectual, and artist Glicéria Tupinambá focuses on recovering Nhengaatu, her people's language, and restoring the practice of crafting Tupinambá mantles—efforts that are intertwined with the struggle for sovereignty and autonomous sustainability of their land. The sacred cloaks worn by shamans, made from the feathers of the scarlet ibis, were brought to colonial European courts in the sixteenth century and some remain in museums today. Tupinambá restarted this tradition in 2006 after centuries of latency, in a sensitive process she calls 'technical cosmos', with the help of photographs, dreams, traditional knowledge of manufacturing fishing nets and twines, and the participation of the living and spiritual community of this territory—a land necessary for the mantles' existence. On the cusp of restitution discussions, this process empowered her people. For *O Quilombismo*, she creates *Tupinambá Ybaka*, reclaiming the ancestral connection of her people to the stars. The works are accompanied by a letter to the audience (see pp. 90–91).

In a residency at HKW in 2024 Glicéria will further her collaboration with other artists and curators, engaging with some of the missing parts to be found in European collections, of the mantle's sacred ritual, and the wisdom emanating from its performance. —A

Works in the exhibition:
Tupinambá Ybaka **[The Tupinambá Sky] (2023), coconut tree bark, cotton thread. Courtesy of the artist; Fernanda Liberti in collaboration with Glicéria Tupinambá,** ***Dancing with the Tupinambá: Mother Bird and Son, Glicéria and Eru, Serra do Padeiro, Bahia, Brazil; Bird View; Thousand in One; Abraço*** **[Hug];** ***Majé*** **[Female Shaman];** ***Poço delemanjá*** **[Iemanjá's Well] (2021), photographic series. Courtesy of the artist**

Tupinambá Ybaka—The Tupinambá Sky

I am Glicéria de Jesus da Silva, also known as Glicéria Tupinambá or Célia Tupinambá. I live in the Indigenous territory of Tupinambá de Olivença in the south of Bahia, Brazil. I am a member of the Indigenous rights movement, I fight to defend my territory and my community, and if I know what I am today, it is because of my territory.

In 2010, because of the struggle for the defense of our lands, I was taken to prison. One day, while being held there, there was a rebellion and we stayed in the courtyard during the night. There was a child there, who was one year and two months old, and when the night came he looked up at the sky and saw the stars. He started to call the people around him to see it, and all of a sudden, when no one was paying attention, he began to dance to the stars. He would spin and jump trying to catch them. I also had my son in my arms, he was just a few months old. While I was there, watching that child discovering the sky for the first time, I realized how much had been taken away from us. They even colonized the sky. I started to ask myself: how is our sky? How is the sky of my people? How is the sky of Indigenous peoples? This question stayed with me. Later, I started to develop and work with the Tupinambá mantle. The mantle also speaks and in a dream it said to me that the mantle was a gift from heaven to the earth, that it held this connection. And while I was making the mesh of the mantle, I realized that mesh is also the mesh of the sky, it is the network of the stars. And so, I observed and looked for that sky even more, every day.

Since I was a child, I had always heard that the *encantados* (ancestral entities) come through a branch of the stars. I had also heard that it was necessary to look at the sky to know if it was going to rain or for how long the rain would last. For everything, the elders told us to look to the sky. As a child, I didn't understand it. I looked at the stars and I didn't understand that the dimming of their brightness symbolized that it was going to rain. When I managed to understand that the stars had this connection to our territory and our knowledge, I decided to return to that knowledge. Because it is important not only in taking back our name, but to look at the function that that knowledge has in the world. This notion was not lost with the older ones.

Travellers and priests through time have recorded the Tupinambá sky. They wrote about the constellation Tuibaé or The Old Man with His Staff. For the Tupinambás, he symbolized the creation of humanity. It was him who carved the first human out of trees. The trees donated the material and he carved us out with his staff.

Then, he handed over the mission to continue the creation of humanity to the *pajé* [shaman], and left to live amongst the stars. He is also an important guide for time demarcation. Besides Tuibaé, there are other constellations such as Tapir's Path, the rhea, the deer, and several other animal representations. Indeed, the earth is represented in the sky.

The constellation known in Brazil as Três Marias, in the Tupinambá language, would be Joykexo. These three stars represent fertility as well as the path of souls and death. They take care of life from its beginning to its end. The elders always spoke of these three stars and they looked at them, prayed to them, and asked them for information. When a season begins to change, they will say whether it's going to rain or going to be sunny. We must look to the stars to see what the climate will be. This is fundamental to us because we do not depend on any technology other than these teachings passed down from the elderly. The Tapir's Path constellation is what guided people through their journeys and helped them to go from one place to another. In that time, they did not have maps, it was through and with the sky that people walked. The stars were a map, a guide, a path.

Every day I try to get closer to these stars, to know them better, to understand them better, to understand their function. Because it's not just a part, but it's a whole. The constellations that appear in our sky also represent our encantados. They are the ones that bring me closer to the mantle, closer to the stars. And I would like for other people to hear this, to be able to understand that there is another sky. I bring these stars in the form of a natural fibre, coconut fibre. As Tuibaé, the old man with his staff, did when using the materials donated by the trees, I asked permission to represent, with care and respect, the Tupinambá sky, the encantados, and our stars. This work is an invitation to look at the sky in another way, from another angle, with another gaze. Like that child who looked at the sky for the first time, who danced to the stars, who tried to hold them in his hand. So I invite each one, each person, to see this sky, and to look for their own.

Glicéria Tupinambá
Serra do Padeiro, 23 January 2023

Translation by Túlio Rosa

1955, Juatuba, Minas Gerais, Brazil, lives in Diamantina, Minas Gerais, Brazil

Eustáquio Neves

Trained as a chemist, Eustáquio Neves began his life as a self-taught photographer in the mid 1980s. Inspired by Arthur Bispo do Rósario, the great Brazilian visual artist who created works of art that he believed to be part of a divine mission, Neves began altering negatives, a technique that became central to his artistic practice. In the forty years since, the autodidact has grappled with the underacknowledged position of Afro-descendants of enslaved people in Brazil. His work captures and manipulates images linked to racial subjugation, intolerance towards Afro-descendant rites, and violence against Black bodies. *Crispim / Encomendador de Almas* depicts the daily life of Crispim, a member of one of the last remaining Baú maroon communities in Minas Gerais established in the spirit of the *quilombos*. Subsistence culture and the maintenance of ancestral rituals through hereditary religious practices remain central to the communities living there today; Crispim, for example, is entrusted with facilitating the transition between the world of the living and the dead. In Neves's work, his presence is made tangible through medicinal herbs and *vissungo*, a form of call and response in a mix of African languages that was sung by Black enslaved miners in Diamantina. —SM

Work in the exhibition:
Crispim / Encomendador de Almas **(2006–22), video installation, double projection, 6' 02"**
Courtesy of the artist

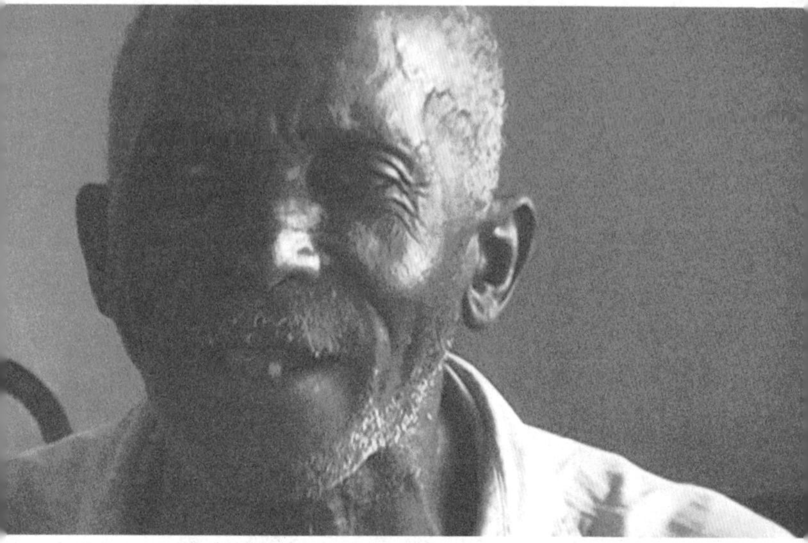

Videostills

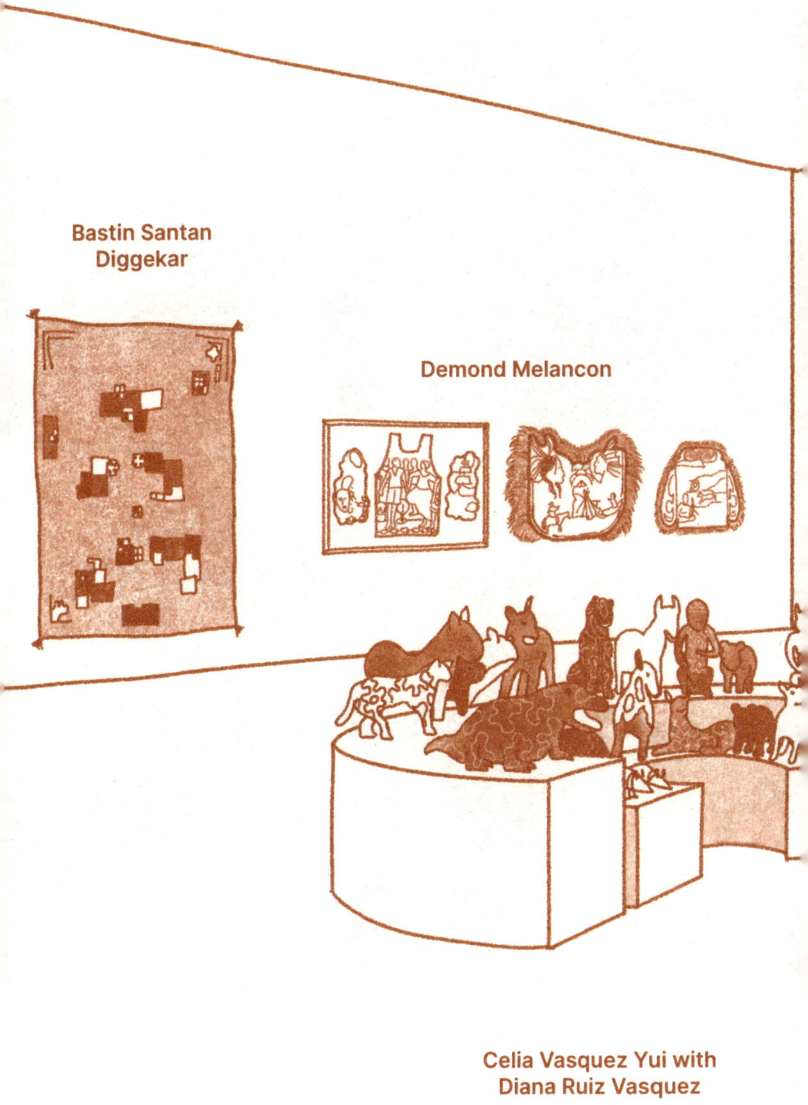
Bastin Santan
Diggekar
Demond Melancon
Celia Vasquez Yui with
Diana Ruiz Vasquez

Truong
Cong Tung
Bernardo Oyarzún

Bastin Santan Diggekar, Shakirambi Ganishab Tattongi, Bibijan Babushab Gunjavathi, Badimabi Gafarsab Ugrani, and Saidambi Imamasab Naik

The Siddi communities across the western coast of India trace their origins from the eastern regions of the African continent, arriving eastwards over the past millennium at various times and in various circumstances: as merchants on the Somali-Indian coastal trade routes (superseded in later centuries by the Swahili-Indian route), as sailors, mercenaries, aristocrats, and as people who were enslaved. The Siddi legacy in India includes royal houses of Bengal, Ahmadnagar, or Janjira, among many other political and military figures. Several Siddi communities thrive today in India, having established casteless and more egalitarian societies than the surrounding mainstream social structures in the country. Women from Siddi communities have developed a quilting textile practice, one that is continuously evolving and morphing, ever refining a stunning language of vibrant abstraction part of no other art historical genealogy. While the pieces are reminiscent of several quilting practices and artists from different Afro-diasporic communities in the Americas, the Siddi quilts are artistic languages developed locally, with various aesthetic and protective strategies, such as the patterns at the corners of the quilt that are meant to function as amulets and forms of ensuring safety. —CC

Quilt by Hattarabi Maulasab Gunjavati is
displayed in Beatriz Nascimento Hall, see p. 202.

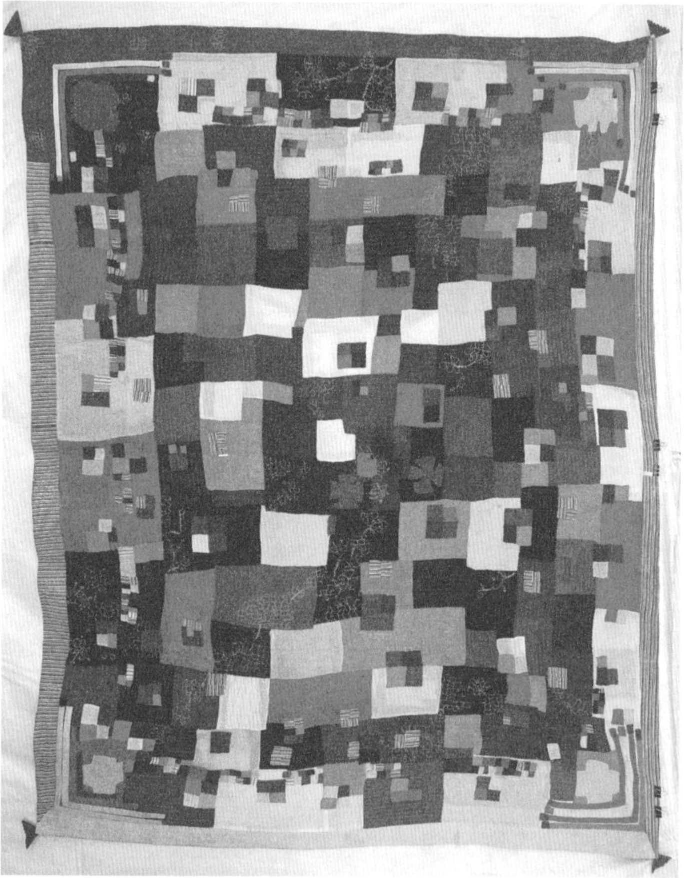

Bastin Santan Diggekar, *Untitled*
Photo: Anitha N Reddy

Works in the exhibition:
Shakirambi Ganishab Tattongi, *Untitled* (2023), textile, hand-stitched siddi kavand with embroidery, 127 × 241 cm; Bibijan Babushab Gunjavathi, *Untitled* (2023), textile, hand-stitched siddi kavand with embroidery, 142 × 226 cm; Badimabi Gafarsab Ugrani, *Untitled* (2023), textile, hand-stitched siddi kavand with embroidery, 135 × 213 cm; Saidambi Imamasab Naik, *Untitled* (2023), textile, hand-stitched siddi kavand with embroidery, 132 × 239 cm; Bastin Santan Diggekar, *Untitled* (2023), textile, hand-stitched siddi kavand with embroidery, 280 × 229 cm. Courtesy of the artists

1978, New Orleans, US,
lives there

Demond Melancon

Ethiopia, Mardi Gras Day 2018. Photo: Gabriel Biencyzcki

Works in the exhibition:
Bras-Coupé (Vest and Dickie) (2016), beading, glass beads, and rhinestones on canvas, framed, 89.5 × 127 cm; *Africa* (2011), beading, glass beads, rhinestones on canvas, framed, 96.5 × 121.9 cm; *Red Cloud & Sitting Bull* (2013), beading, glass beads, rhinestones on canvas, 137.2 × 165.1 cm. Courtesy of Arthur Roger Gallery, New Orleans

***Jah Defender*, Mardi Gras Day 2021. Photo: Ryan Hodgson-Rigsbee**

As a Big Chief, Demond Melancon is one of the carriers of the more than 200-year-old tradition of the Black Masking culture of New Orleans, a unique subculture dating back to the 1800s when Native Americans helped enslaved African runaways, forging an intercultural friendship that includes rituals, craftsmanship, and spirituality. For decades he has been developing an art practice based on the beading techniques he learned as a Black Masker. He creates Black Masking suits for ceremonial and ritual events such as Mardi Gras and St Joseph's Night, and has also developed a portraiture series, in both cases using only needle and thread to apply glass beads to canvas. The life-size suits comprise many individual beaded patches stitched together, the final form framed by coloured ostrich plumes. Each of the suits reflects on historical and mythical accounts, transferring them into a collective visual narrative that centres Black subjects, their own history, struggles, philosophy, and knowledge, thereby confronting stereotypical representations of Black identity. *Bras-Coupé*, for example, is dedicated to a mythical runaway and depicts figures at Congo Square, where dance and trading were possible to obtain the spiritual and material resources necessary for freedom. In a similar vein, another one of Melancon's works, *Jah Defender* (2020), was placed on top of where a confederate monument once stood. —AOW/A

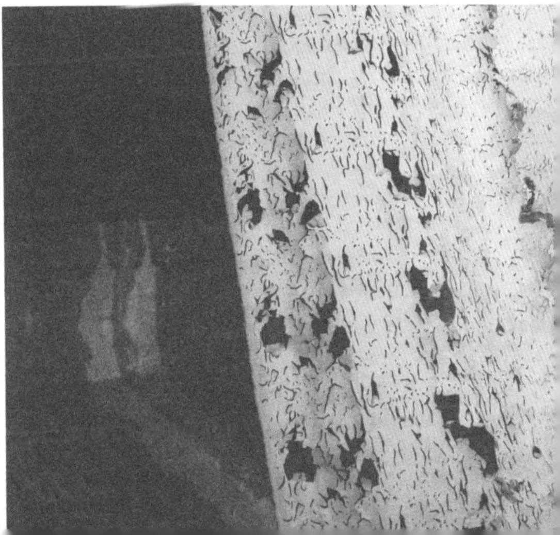

Detail. Photos:
Truong Cong Tung

1986, Dak Lak, Vietnam, lives in Ho Chi Minh City, Vietnam

Truong Cong Tung

Truong Cong Tung was born in the Central Highlands of Vietnam to a family belonging to the majority Kinh community who had recently moved to the lands of the Jrai Indigenous community—a circumstance that has significantly impacted his views on his artistic practice and political engagements. Truong is influenced by traditional spiritual practices of Vietnam, some of which are shaped by Buddhism, to investigate modes of being with non-humans that emerge within these traditions, including plants, insects, and spirits. In *Blind Map*, he invites a colony of termites to occupy a length of canvas and presents the traces of their vigorous activity in a form that is both random and repetitive as the canvas is unwrapped. Through this process, a transfiguration takes place where the artist becomes termite, and the termite becomes a painter, creating a space of indistinct identity across species. —CC

Work in the exhibition:
Blind Map (2013), canvas roll eaten by termites, 600 × 150 cm. Courtesy of Post Vidai Collection, Saigon and Geneva

1960, Pucallpa, Ucayali, Peru, lives in Yarinacocha in the Peruvian Amazon

Celia Vasquez Yui with Diana Ruiz Vasquez

Artist, Indigenous territorial sovereignty activist, and political representative of the Shipibo People of Peru, Celia Vasquez Yui's practice centres ceramics with zoomorphic features that draw from the Shipibo-Conibo visual tradition. *The Council of the Mother Spirits of the Animals* is a collaboration with the Shipibo Conibo Center and features sculptures of animal spirits represented as jaguars, snakes, armadillos, and crocodiles, among others. Highlighting the creative and political potential of all living manifestations of the land, they are presented in an amphitheatre and are accompanied by a soundscape available online. The sonic component of the work incorporates a recording of an ayahuasca ceremony for the planet conducted by members of the Shipibo Union of Ancestral Healers (ASOMASHK) as well as sounds from the Peruvian Amazon, fostering a non-verbal communion with nature. Vasquez Yui keeps alive the ancestral custom of mixing pieces of broken ceramics with clay from the riverbanks from where they originated. She also integrates rituals such as fasting, lighting tobacco while firing, and incorporating her granddaughter's hair into the paint brushes she uses. Through her work, the artist invokes and evokes an understanding of ecology and interspecies healing to confront the spiritual and ecological maladies of the contemporary world. —RC/A

Scan to listen to *Asomashk, A Ceremony for the Mother Spirits of the Animals* (2021).

Works in the exhibition:
The Council of the Mother Spirits of the Animals (2020/2023), installation, coil-built pre-fire slip-painted clay, vegetal resins; *Asomashk, A Ceremony for the Mother Spirits of the Animals* (2021), sound recording, 2'37". Courtesy of the artists and Shipibo Conibo Center, New York

The Council of the Mother Spirits of the Animals, exhibition view, Salon 94, New York, 2022. Photos: Elisabeth Bernstein. Courtesy of the artists; Shipibo Conibo Center, New York; and Salon 94, New York

1963, Los Muermos, Región de los Lagos, Chile, lives in Colicheo, Cabrero, Bío-Bío, Chile

Bernardo Oyarzún

Through his artistic practice Bernardo Oyarzún confronts experiences of racism, notably in the context of the resistance of the Indigenous Mapuche ('people of the land') culture in Chile and Argentina. Of Mapuche descent himself, Oyarzún has created works since the 1990s that revitalize popular practices and aesthetics, asserting the ancestral and contemporary Indigenous knowledge that they impart—through craft, orality, culinary arts, rituals, and festivities. In his large sculpture *Kilombo: Piwuchen*, the mythological shape-shifting figure Piwuchen takes the allegorical form of a parade float, coming to life in the world of Carnival. The colourful snake-like creature is based on recent stories told by inhabitants of southern Chile in the Mapuche and Chiloé territories, thereby embodying the Indigenous imaginary that lives on through different generations via orality. Following his earlier work *Kilombo* (2012), Oyarzún recalls the African origin of *quilombo*—meaning 'war camp' from the Kimbundu word *kilombo*—connecting the cultural resistance of Indigenous people and Afro-descendants against (neo)colonialism within and across continents. Playful, contemporary, and historical, Oyarzún's practice always contains a story, which the viewer may pass on, generating change and joy within their own communities. —PG

Commissioned by Haus der Kulturen der Welt (HKW), co-produced by Bernardo Oyarzún and HKW, and realized with the support of the Ministerio de las Culturas, las Artes y el Patrimonio | Gobierno de Chile (Ministry of Cultures, Arts and Heritage | Government of Chile), 2023.

***El Médan*, performance by Bernardo Oyarzún during the opening weekend, see p. 257.**

Model for *Kilombo: Piwuchen*.
Photo: Bernardo Oyarzún

Work in the exhibition:
Kilombo: Piwuchen (2023), sculpture, papier marché, diverse materials, 3 × 5 × 2 m
Courtesy of the artist

Antonio Jose Guzman
& Iva Jankovic

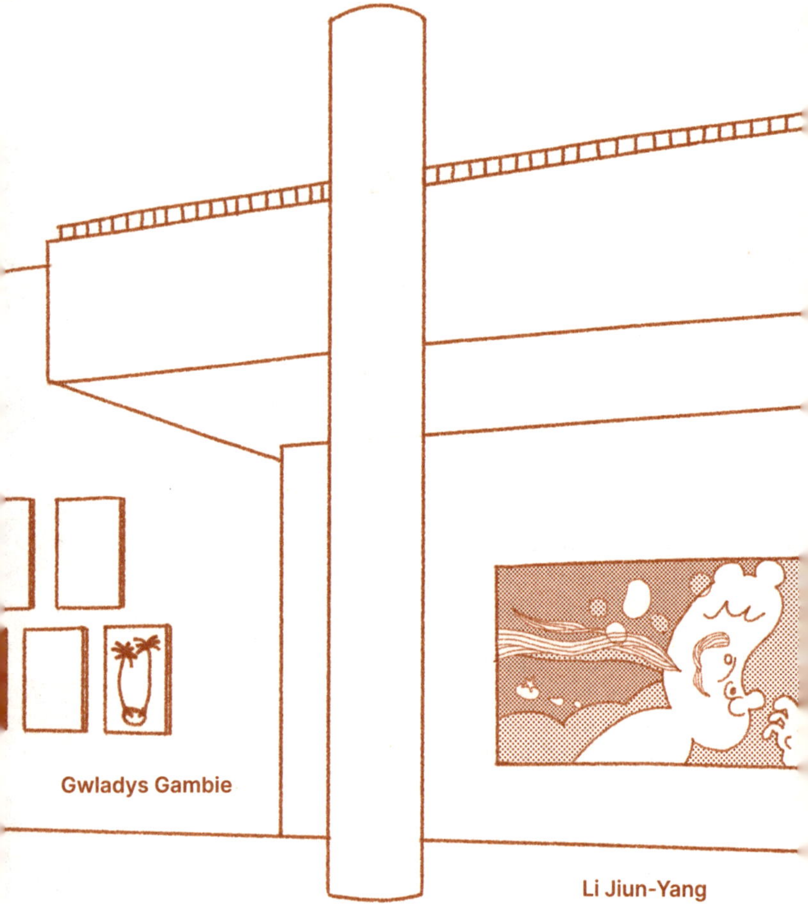
Gwladys Gambie
Li Jiun-Yang

1971, Panama City, Panama, lives in Amsterdam, The Netherlands; Gujarat, India; and Panama City, Panama

Antonio Jose Guzman

Visual artist, researcher, dub poet, and Afrofuturist Antonio Jose Guzman's multidisciplinary works tackle social justice issues and notions of community, identity, and ancestry by engaging with the colonial history of textiles, memory, and time. He is inspired by diasporic identities and centres the positive role of migration and community engagement. In *Transatlantic Stargate,* Guzman reinterprets the transatlantic colonial history of indigo blue textiles to interrogate the Netherlands' history of slavery and the country's colonial practices throughout the Black Atlantic. These textiles, suffused with symbolic, spiritual, and historical significance, of stories and memories of diaspora, ancient spirits, and sacred powers, became valuable during the transatlantic trade of enslaved people. *Transatlantic Stargate* is based on the installation and performance project *Messengers of the Sun* (2023) that Guzman co-conceived with Iva Jankovic. For *O Quilombismo*, Guzman presents a new arrangement of newly made textiles that uses the same ancient indigo block printing technique called *Ajrakh* from their previous work, made in collaboration with Sufiyan Ismail Khatri and his team in Ajrakhpur, India. Ajrakh, which is 4,000 years old, is more than a printing technique; consistent with the spirit of *quilombismo*, Ajrakh is a way of life and learning, with knowledge and practice orally passed down through generations. —RC

Commissioned by Haus der Kulturen der Welt (HKW), co-produced by Antonio Jose Guzman, Iva Jankovic, and HKW, and realized with the support of The Mondriaan Fund, Amsterdam, 2023.

1979, Ruma, at that time
Yugoslavia, lives in Amsterdam,
The Netherlands and Gujarat, India

& Iva Jankovic

Model for *Transatlantic Stargate*. Photo: © Guzman & Jankovic Atelier GF Workstation Amsterdam, 2023

Work in the exhibition:
Transatlantic Stargate (2023), indigo dyed textiles, 5 × 5 m. Courtesy of the artists

1988, Fort-de-France, Martinique,
lives there

Gwladys Gambie

Manman Chadwon to Manman Chadwon (2023), ink on paper, 75 × 110 cm © VG Bild-Kunst, Bonn 2023

Martinican artist Gwladys Gambie celebrates the Black female body, sensually and mythologically questioning oppression, control, stereotypes, norms, and representation. *Poetic of Celebration* depicts the poetics of the feminized body in ways that free it from the constraints of colonialism, patriarchy, and racism. It consists of six new drawings rooted in African mythologies and traditions in Martinique and inspired by Manman Chadwon, Goddess of Sea Urchins and descendant of the Afro-Caribbean deity and goddess of the ocean, Manman Dlo. Manman Chadwon is Gambie's alter ego—a metamorphosing and emancipatory figure who spiritually connects the artist with nature and her African ancestry. Bodies, flora, and fauna intermingle in Gambie's drawings, where the colour red features prominently. It represents blood used in rituals, connecting ancestors with the living, and renders present those who have been lost through centuries of enslavement. Gambie's art liberates the feminized body by bridging generations, continents, temporalities, ancestors, humans, and nature. —RC

Commissioned by Haus der Kulturen der Welt (HKW), co-produced by Gwladys Gambie and HKW, 2023.

Work in the exhibition:
***Poetic of Celebration* (2023), drawings, ink on paper, mixed media, 75 × 110 cm each**
Courtesy of the artist

1967, Taitung, Taiwan, lives in
Taichung, Taiwan

Li Jiun-Yang

Detail

This large-scale canvas is representative of Li Jiun-Yang's distinctive practice and engagement with traditional Taiwanese art forms, diverse religious representations, and vernacular culture on the island. The son of a movie poster painter, Li has also worked on movie posters, as well as temple paintings, calligraphy, Taiwanese glove puppets, and multimedia installations. Hailing from southern Taiwan, a distinctive cultural environment influenced by Taiwanese Indigenous people and Hoklo (descendants of the first Chinese migrants on the island arriving from the seventeenth century onwards and speaking the Minnan variety of Chinese languages), Li promotes a Taiwanese identity distinct from the Chinese Nationalist idea that sees Taiwan as part of a homogeneous Chinese cultural world. In the first centuries of Chinese migration to the island, both religious and political life revolved around vernacular temples, which were connected in horizontal structures—a system that provided forms of organization that eluded centralized political control. The world inhabiting Li's canvas is a reflection of both the characters and the general spirit of boundless imagination born in those centuries of parallel political modes in Taiwan, prior to Japanese occupation. With the current spectre of imperialist Chinese takeover looming over the island, that idealized moment of local political imagination is being revisited in the public sphere. —CC

Work in the exhibition:
Fairy-Fairy-Fairy 35 **(2011), painting, acrylic on canvas, 509 × 144 cm. Courtesy of the artist**

Masimba Hwati
Grada Kilomba

Shakirambi Ganishab Tattongi,
Bibijan Babushab Gunjavathi,
Badimabi Gafarsab Ugrani and
Saidambi Imamasab Naik

1982, Harare, Zimbabwe, lives in
Vienna, Austria and Michigan, US

Masimba Hwati

With assembled found objects, Masimba Hwati creates sculptures to which a new life is insufflated with the breath of invited sonic makers. He examines post-colonial subjects and contributes to broader reflections around artistic practice as a vehicle of change and a tool for rewriting history. The second *Chimurenga* (revolutionary struggle) of today's Republic of Zimbabwe took place from the early 1960s to 1979 and led to the country's liberation from colonial rule in 1980. Inspired by the resistance and resilience of imprisoned freedom fighters, Hwati highlights their acts of flight in these sculptures as crucial tools used for survival. The radio specifically was a central device for resistance struggles in Zimbabwe and other African geographies and is described by Hwati as 'an apparatus of care and healing for the people that allowed the freedom fighters to act in between the cracks and gaps of the ruling system'. Smuggling radios, newspaper clippings, and love and solidarity messages into loaves of bread became an improvised gesture performed by co-fighters and loved ones who kept the hope alive for those who were cut off from society. —MHP

Bread Scores, performance by Masimba Hwati and friends Laura Anh Thu Dang, Luka Mukhavele, Lefteris Krysalis on Sunday, 4 June, 15:00, see p. 270.

Works in the exhibition:
Dzikamunhenga 3 (2022) sculpture, mixed media 126 × 50 × 25 cm; *Dzikamunhenga 4* (2022), sculpture, mixed media 120 × 62 × 40 cm
Courtesy of the artist and Tiwani Contemporary, London and Lagos

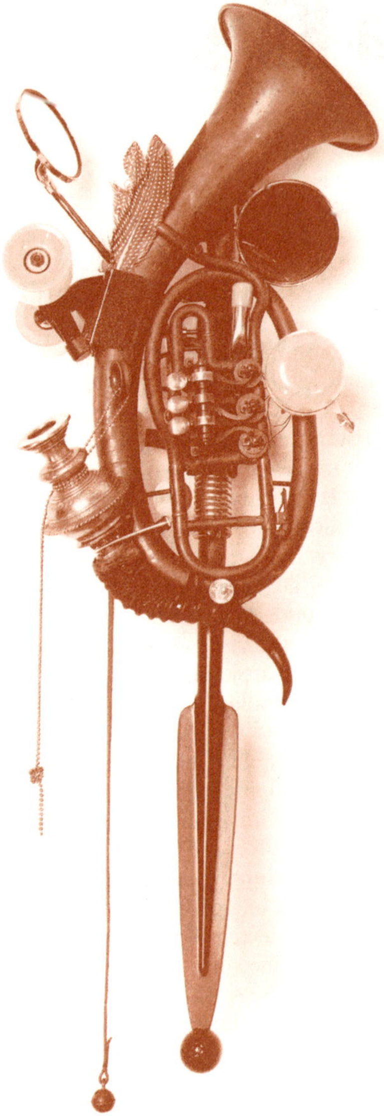

Dzikamunhenga 4. Photo: Kafeela Ade

1968, Lisbon, Portugal, lives in Berlin, Germany

Grada Kilomba

Explorations of memory, trauma, and post-colonialism are central to Grada Kilomba's work, which interrogates knowledge systems and confronts the consequences of colonialism through interdisciplinary formats. The subversion of linearity in her work offers spirituality as an alternative system of understanding and communing. *Table of Goods* makes use of earth—the one and utmost repository of all beings—to form a pyramid of soil revisiting the brutality of slavery. Indented with pockets that accommodate coffee, sugar, and cocoa, and surrounded by candles, the work investigates the violence that facilitates modern pleasures. Simultaneously, Kilomba's installation employs storytelling as a medium that looks beyond trauma and creates spaces for healing through ritual and remembrance. She uses the term 'unspeakable' as a metaphor for trauma and the colonial wound, explaining how 'colonialism is a wound that has never been properly treated, an infected wound that always hurts, sometimes infects and sometimes bleeds'. The use of earth here also acts as a connector, drawing a strong line of solidarity towards acts of resistance and resilience related to issues of land also presented in the frame of *O Quilombismo*. —DMV/MHP

Table of Goods, installation view, MAAT, Lisbon, 2017. Photo: Bruno Lopes

Work in the exhibition:
Table of Goods (2017), installation, soil, coffee beans, ground coffee, cocoa, dark chocolate, sugar, white candles, dimensions vary
Courtesy of the artist

Forough Farrokzhad Garden

p. 126 Temitayo Ogunbiyi

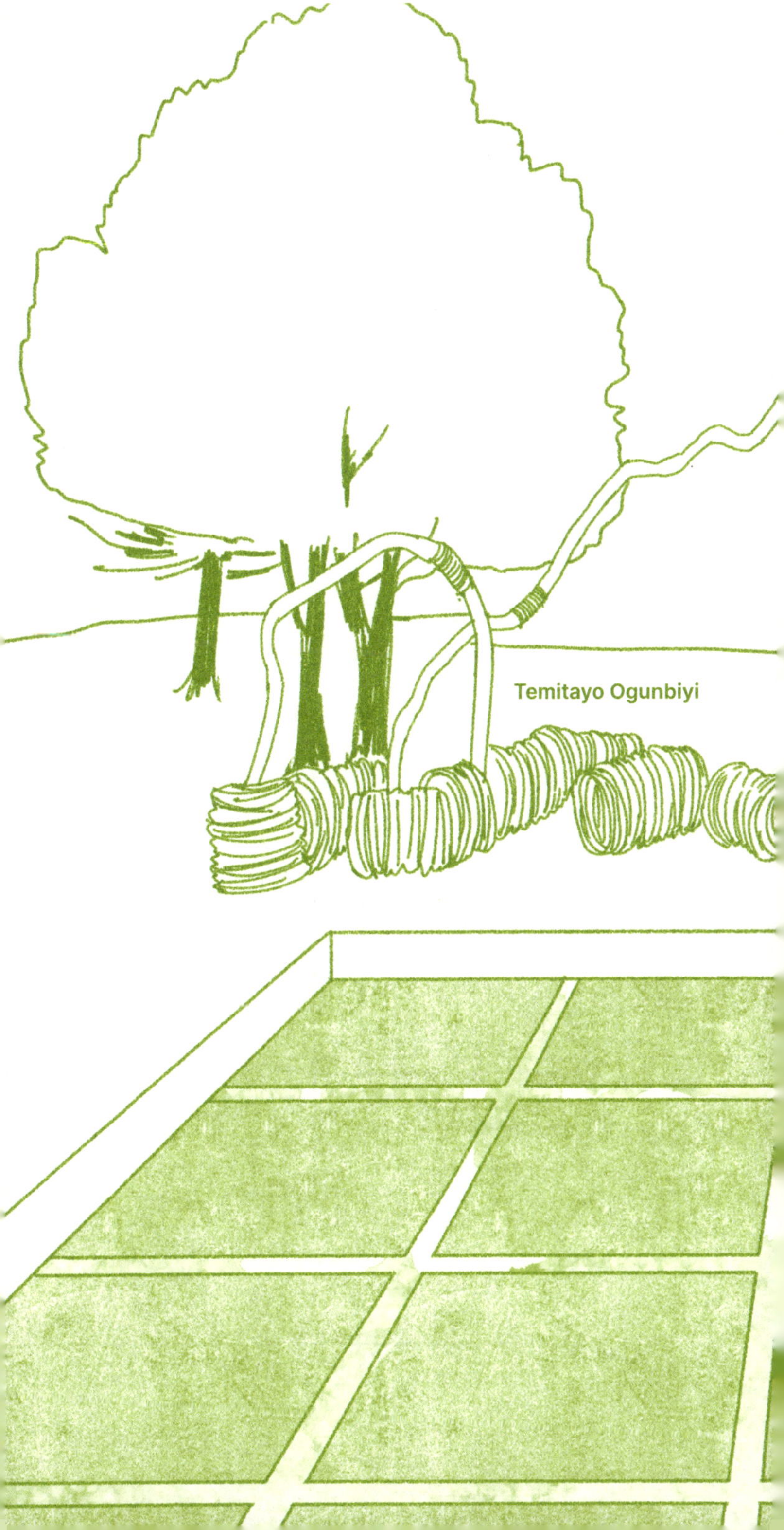
Temitayo Ogunbiyi

1984, New York, US,
lives in Lagos, Nigeria

Temitayo Ogunbiyi

The practice of Nigerian visual artist Temitayo Ogunbiyi moves between drawing, painting, sculpture, and installation. Often producing works that are in reaction to global and current events, she places her artistic practice in dialogue with anthropological histories and botanical cultures closely intertwined with a colonial legacy. Her works on paper have expanded in form and scale as her practice has evolved, materializing into sculptural propositions. Shaped most regularly like routes or maps, they reflect the artist's interest in the historical conditions that have determined the movements of people and materials across geographies. For her first public installation in Naples, Italy, Ogunbiyi created *You will play in the everyday, running* (2020), a playground structure that makes a plea for unregulated movement amidst a politic to police and thereby provides a free space for children to play and interact with her work without set restrictions. Drawing upon this and thinking about the notion of freedom for all beings, she has designed a resting area within the *O Quilombismo* exhibition which invites visitors to sit, rest, and connect with the outdoor environment. Ogunbiyi's installation *You will forge paths beyond your grandmother's imaginings* stands as a gift to the guests of HKW and opens up the space by creating a connection between the inside and out. —EFB

Commissioned by Haus der Kulturen der Welt (HKW), co-produced by Temitayo Ogunbiyi and HKW, 2023.

Work in the exhibition:
You will forge paths beyond your grandmother's imaginings (2023), seating area, Manila rope, stainless steel, concrete, dimensions vary
Courtesy of the artist

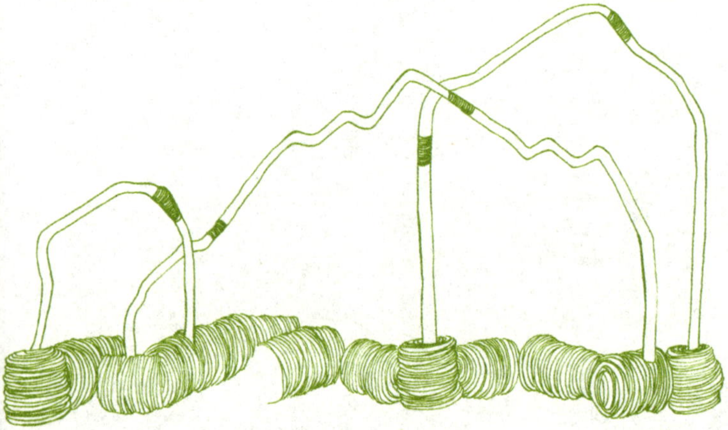

Artist sketch, pencil and pen on herbarium paper, 42 × 30 cm

Bessie Head Foyer & Magnus Hirschfeld Bar

Anand Patwardhan

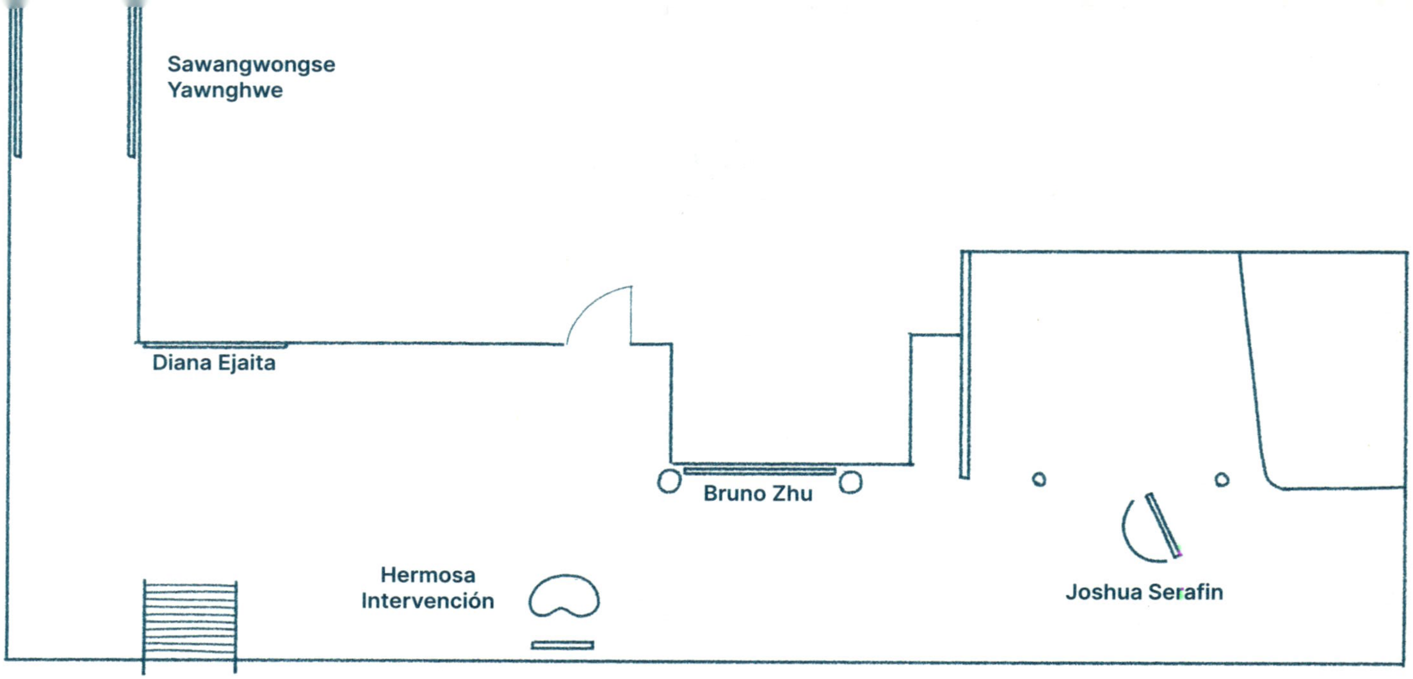
Sawangwongse
Yawnghwe
Diana Ejaita
Bruno Zhu
Hermosa
Intervención
Joshua Serafin

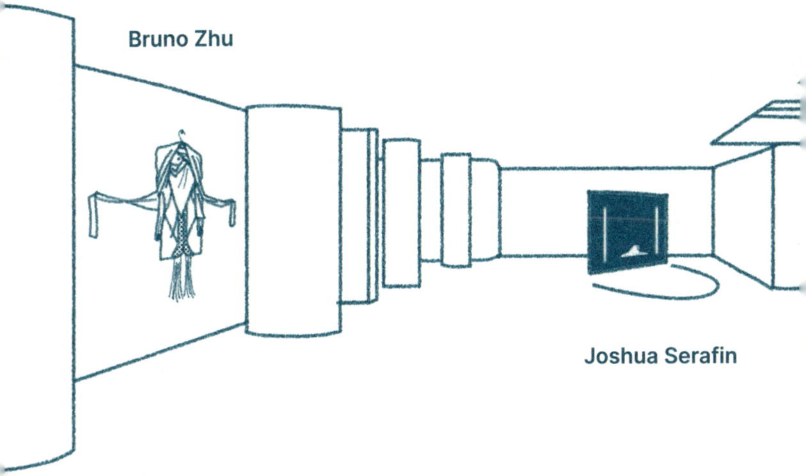
Bruno Zhu
Joshua Serafin

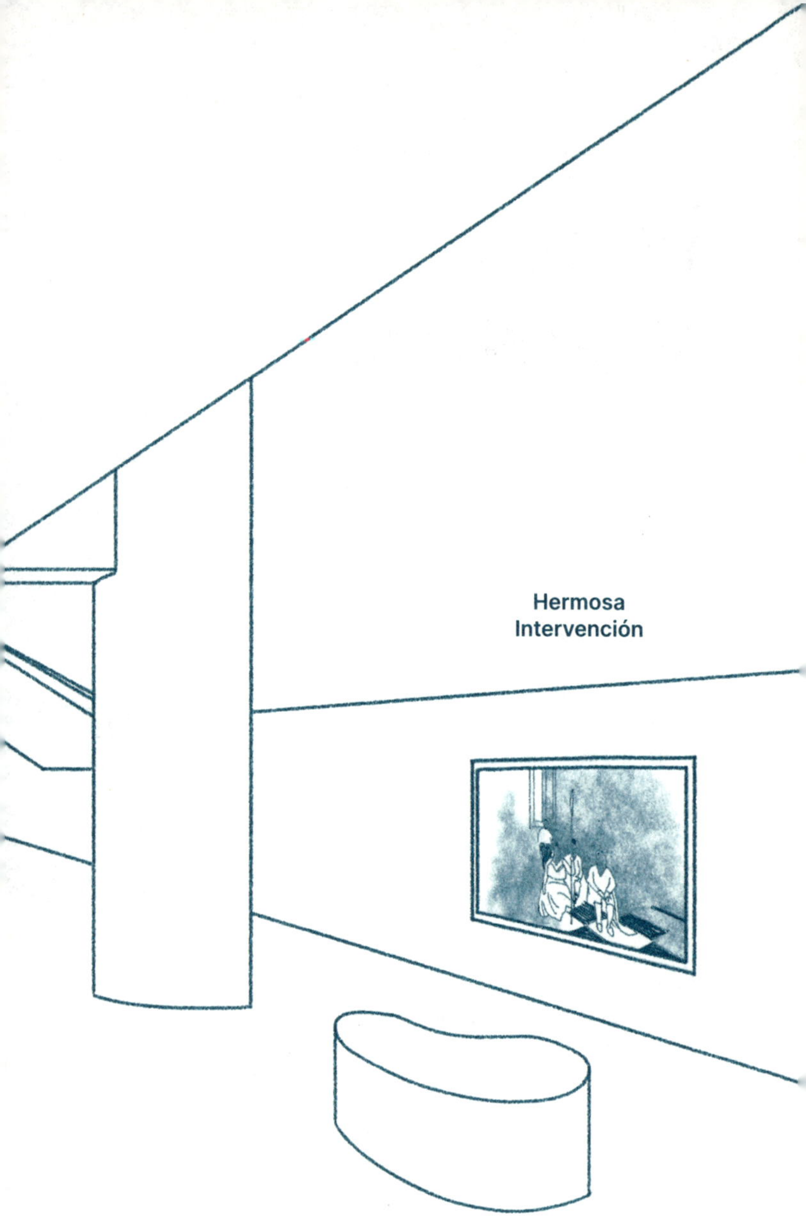
Hermosa
Intervención

Hermosa Intervención

Hermosa Intervención is a collective of Afro-Uruguayan women founded in 2020 that came together to reconstruct and perform the history of Afro-Latinas through the project, *El Museo Afroviviente*. By investigating and restaging the historiography of women of African descent who have been vital to the anti-racist cause and in advocating for the rights of Afro-descendant, Indigenous, migrant, and LGBTQ+ populations in Abya Yala, Hermosa Intervención disseminates stories of the African diaspora otherwise neglected by neo-colonial narratives and rendered invisible by educational systems. As a practice based on the power of storytelling and corporeality, their interventions are ignited through performance, spoken word, body paint, sound, and installation. They carry out interventions in several institutions across Montevideo in central and peripheral neighbourhoods and tour Uruguay to reach out to various communities. In the collective, *hermosa* (beautiful) refers to the pride of their own bodies and stories, since the life experience of each member is interwoven into the stories they bring to life. Thus, Hermosa Intervención celebrates 'the body as a transmitter of black histories'. Distancing themselves from the Eurocentric, object-oriented museum, they invite the public to a *living* experience and to carry their stories with us long after. —PG

Commissioned by Haus der Kulturen der Welt (HKW), co-produced by Hermosa Intervención and HKW, 2023.

The Hermosa Intervención collective
Photo: Lucia Coppola

Work in the exhibition:
El Museo Afroviviente (2023), documentary video, 20'
Courtesy of Hermosa Intervención

Bruno Zhu

1991, Porto, Portugal, lives in Amsterdam, The Netherlands and Viseu, Portugal

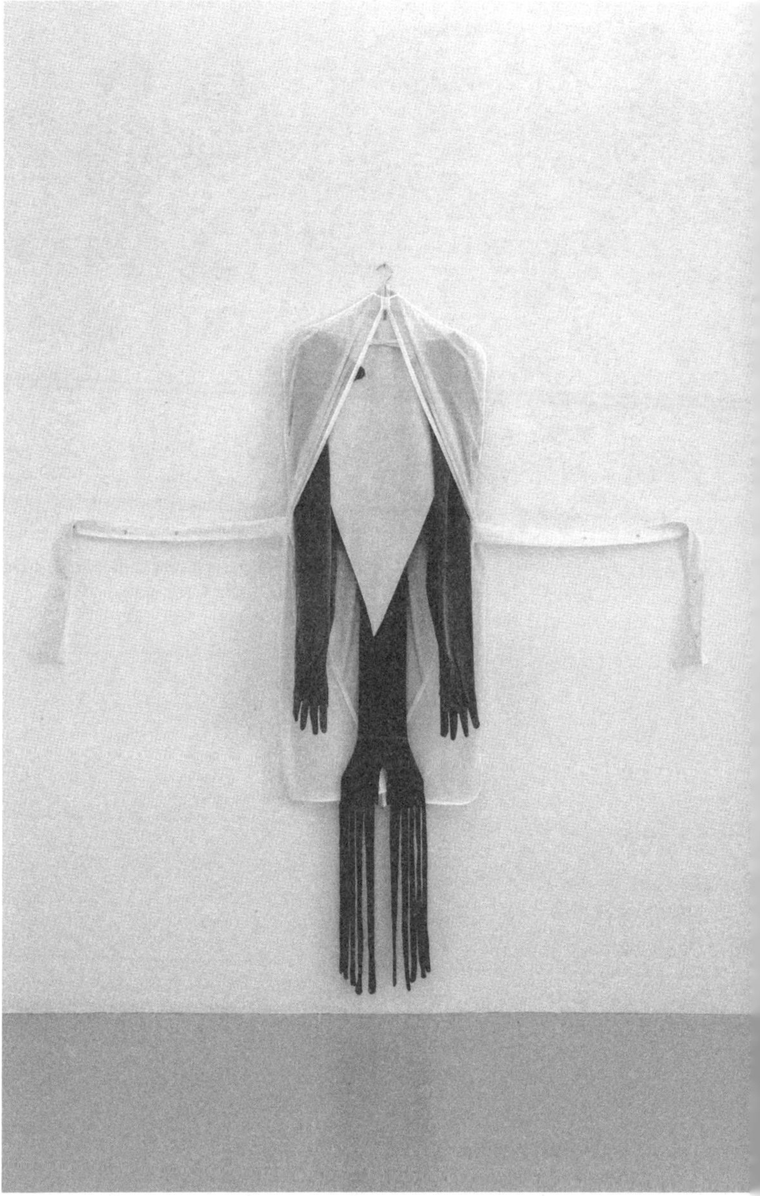

Photo: Sebastian Black. Courtesy of the artist and Kimberly-Klark, Queens, New York

Bruno Zhu was trained in fashion design and developed his artistic practice at A Maior, his parents' shop selling Chinese fashion and household wares in Viseu, Portugal, where they migrated to from China before Zhu was born. A Maior not only provided the impetus for his work, he also curated shows there with its employees as well as local and international artists. Zhu's practice to date has been diverse, encompassing textile, photography, installation, and writing. It engages, albeit subtly, with an equally diverse set of themes including, among others, desire, consumption, commodified and racialized selves, objectification, and autobiography. Recently, issues surrounding identity politics, racism, and Portugal's colonial history have become an urgent aspect of Zhu's art and writing in light of his own experiences in the Portuguese art scene. Fashion, too, continues to play a central role, with the artist using clothing to explore failure and the death of lives, performance, movement, and goods and also as a vessel for reincarnation. *Man in the Closet* is one such work that evokes the tensions of (in)visibility and a refusal to be boxed into specific categories or identities, while functioning as an almost totemic figure—one derived from the artist's personal experience and incorporating references to queer culture more broadly. —RC

Work in the exhibition:
Man in the Closet **(2017–23), textile work, men's trousers, wool socks, canvas, cheesecloth, dimensions vary**
Courtesy of the artist

1995, Bacolod City, Philippines, lives in Brussels, Belgium and Manila, Philippines

Joshua Serafin

Unpacking the societal effects and psychological and physical fractures caused by colonialism and imperialism, artist/performance maker Joshua Serafin turns towards queer and Indigenous embodiment and imaginativeness as a way of negotiating and reclaiming a sense of displacement, not-belonging, and in-betweenness. Serafin's approach is reminiscent of the performative operation of marginalized peoples so potently described by theorist José Esteban Muñoz as 'disidentification'. Anchored in the context of their own research and positionality, in *Miss* (2020), for example, Serafin investigates the physical vocabularies and power relations of transgender beauty pageantry in the Philippines, tracing its religious and colonial predicaments as manifested in its performance of class, race, and gender. For *O Quilombismo*, the artist presents *Void*, a film that is part of the trilogy *Cosmological Gangbang* (2021–24), referencing a total absence and the potential to become anything—a situation queer subjectivities are placed in when confronted with their erasure from both historical and future existence. *Void* is a duality: a non-binary, brown-bodied, ghostly deity character and alter identity, and its own representation or lack of it. It affirms and departs from itself, and offers refuge in Indigenous ancestrality and its queerness, in the modus of myth characteristic of the fluid, pre-colonial Filipino gender belief systems, and in the spirituality passed down through intergenerational oral knowledge. —A

A live performance of *Void* takes place on 23 June. For further information visit www.hkw.de.

Video stills

Work in the exhibition:
Void (2022), video installation, 10'
Film Direction, Cinematography:
Brandon Relucio and Davide Belotti
Sound Design: Alex Zhang Huntai
Courtesy of the artist

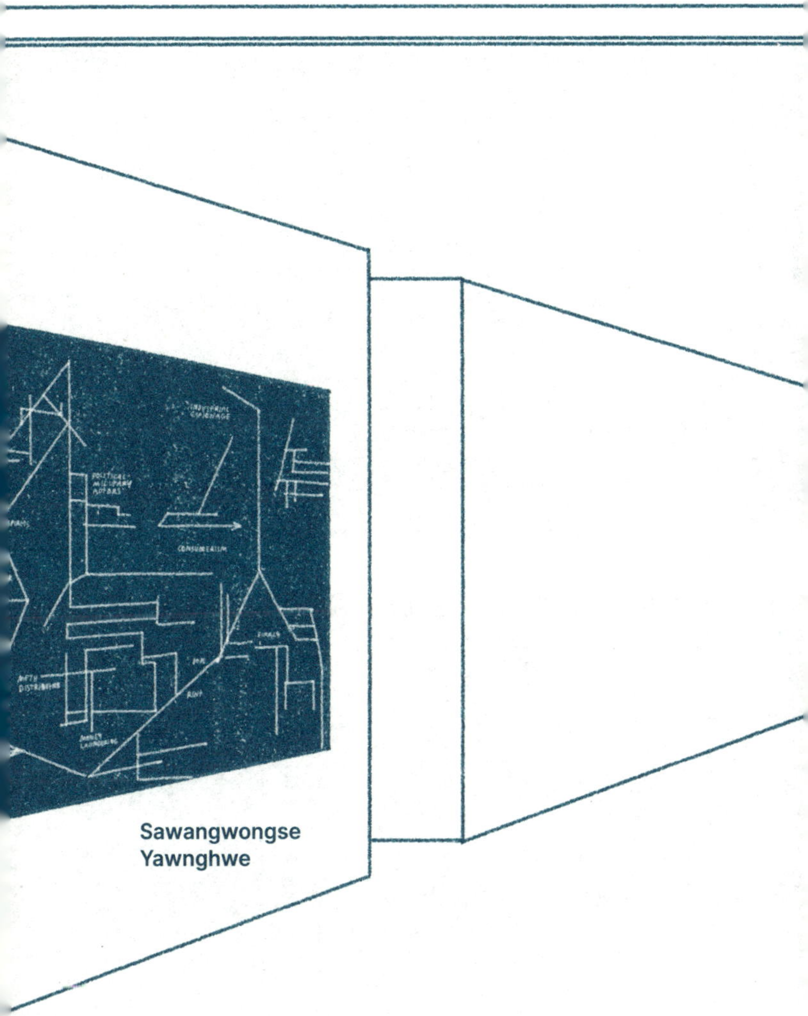
Sawangwongse
Yawnghwe

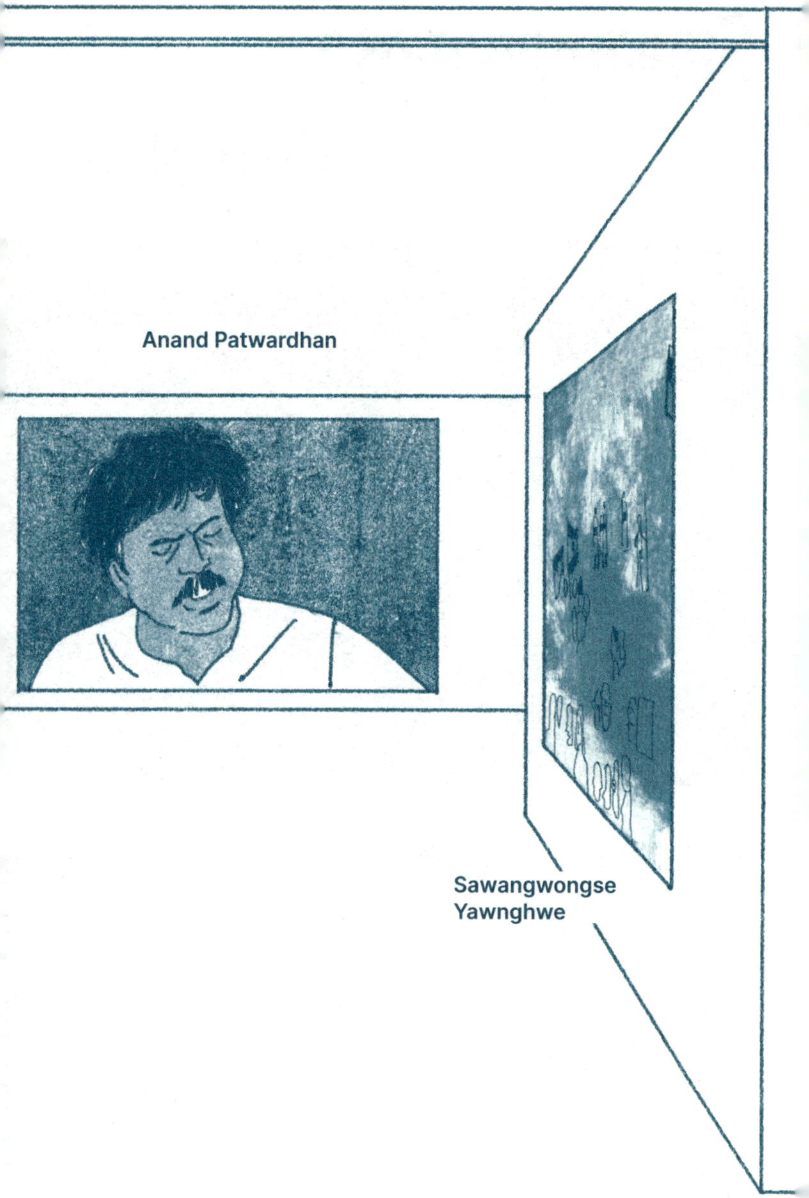
Anand Patwardhan
Sawangwongse Yawnghwe

1971, Shan State, Burma, lives in
Zutphen, The Netherlands

Sawangwongse Yawnghwe

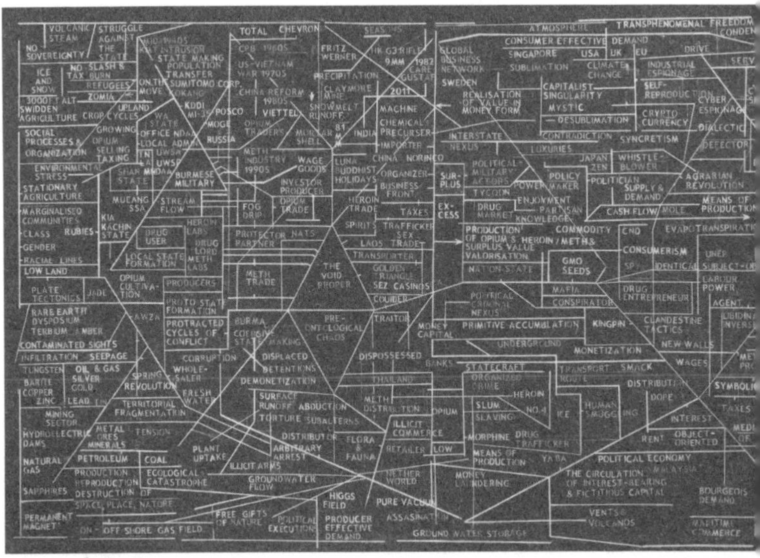

Top: *The Opium Parallax II*. Bottom: *The Rangoon Massacre (The Ides of March)*.
Photos: Courtesy of the artist

Sawangwongse Yawnghwe was born in the Shan State (Myanmar). A descendant of the Yawnghwe royal family of Shan, Yawnghwe's grandfather was Sao Shwe Thaik, the first president of the Union of Burma (1948–62) after the country gained independence from Britain in 1948. Shwe Thaik died in prison following the 1962 military coup by General Ne Win. Since then, Yawnghwe's family has lived in exile. Yawnghwe's painting and installation practice engages politics with reference to his family history and current and historical events in Burma/Myanmar, having been one of the most vocal voices from the country to condemn the Rohingya genocide. More recently, he has engaged with the national uprising following the 2021 military coup. *The Rangoon Massacre (The Ides of March)* is an idealized representation of this popular swell refusing military rule, in all its diversity and in spite of all its other conflicts. *The Opium Parallax II* maps out the many levels of connections that define power structures throughout Myanmar's different regions and across its borders, in other mountainous regions of South East Asia where systems of agriculture and political organization have built a long history of resistance and forms of living together outside of state and imperial control. —CC

Works in the exhibition:
The Opium Parallax II
(2023), painting, acrylic on linen, 225 × 400 cm;
The Rangoon Massacre (The Ides of March)
(2023), painting, acrylic on linen, 225 × 340 cm
Courtesy of the artist

Commissioned by Haus der Kulturen der Welt (HKW), co-produced by Sawangwongse Yawnghwe and HKW, 2023.

1950, Mumbai, at that time Bombay,
India, lives in India

Anand Patwardhan

Detail from a religious poster depicting the Hindu god Hanuman.

We Are Not Your Monkeys is an energy-charged protest song against the Hindu caste hierarchy, written by the Dalit activists Daya Pawar and Sambhaji Bhagat in cooperation with the film-maker Anand Patwardhan. In the video, Bhagat is shown performing the song in a village square, accompanied by choir and percussion, with great intensity. The lyrics deconstruct *Ramayana*, one of the most important Hindu epics, from the perspective of the Dalits: a musical outcry against systematic suppression and contempt for human rights, against rulers who exercise control over the writing of history and depict the Dalits as demons or untouchables. 'But we were the aborigines of this land, listen to our story', sings Bhagat, who also attacks the patriarchy. The sharp-tongued critique is directed against the *Manusmriti*, an ancient Hindu legal text which prohibitively restricts the rights of women. The documentation of the performance is interspersed with racist depictions showing Dalits as apes. Such images are included not simply to reproduce their abhorrent discrimination but to tear them to shreds in verses of the song. —CS

Work in the exhibition:
***We Are Not Your Monkeys* (1996),**
video installation, 5' 19"
Courtesy of the artist

Beatriz Nascimento Hall

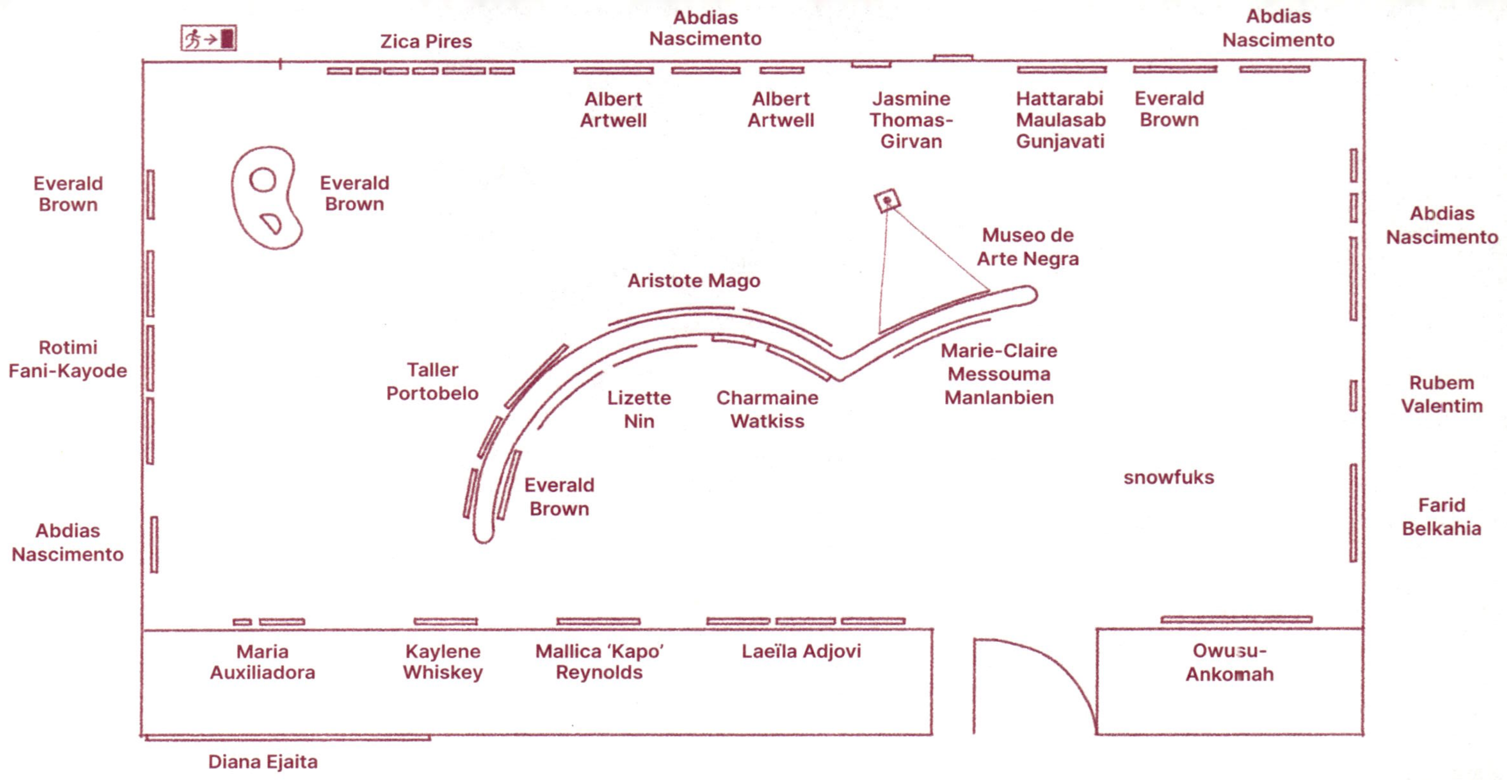
Zica Pires
Abdias Nascimento
Abdias Nascimento
Albert Artwell
Albert Artwell
Jasmine Thomas-Girvan
Hattarabi Maulasab Gunjavati
Everald Brown
Everald Brown
Everald Brown
Abdias Nascimento
Museo de Arte Negra
Aristote Mago
Rotimi Fani-Kayode
Taller Portobelo
Lizette Nin
Charmaine Watkiss
Marie-Claire Messouma Manlanbien
Rubem Valentim
Everald Brown
snowfuks
Farid Belkahia
Abdias Nascimento
Maria Auxiliadora
Kaylene Whiskey
Mallica 'Kapo' Reynolds
Laeïla Adjovi
Owusu-Ankomah
Diana Ejaita

Diana Ejaita

1985, Cremona, Italy, lives in Milan, Italy; Berlin, Germany; and Lagos, Nigeria

Diana Ejaita

Diana Ejaita's practice encompasses installation, illustration, and textile design to reinvigorate visual storytelling traditions of her African lineage. As a Nigerian-Italian diasporic artist, Ejaita's works are concerned with shaping notions of belonging while also revitalizing aesthetic genealogies from the African continent. This oscillation between worlds is reflected in her visual reinterpretation of stories, such as those by Nigerian authors Amos Tutuola and Chinua Achebe, or narrative techniques found in West African textiles. Working with recordings made during residencies in Nigeria and Burkina Faso, Ejaita centres the intergenerational power of stories passed on via oral traditions. For *O Quilombismo*, the artist has created a mural with a series of interlaced figures engaged in the movements of storytelling. Bodies are recurring motifs in this series, emerging and transforming across the pictorial space. Akin to the West African narratives Ejaita engages with, symbols also play an important role in her work, acting as bridges to spiritual dimensions. With its magic-based fable landscapes, the mural summons visitors to look beyond the visual and rather engage with the ancestral channels it opens. —EFB/PG

Commissioned by Haus der Kulturen der Welt (HKW), co-produced by Diana Ejaita and HKW, 2023.

Work in the exhibition:
Bodies, Tales, and Landscapes. Progression III (2023), poster prints, 42 × 59.4 cm each
Courtesy of the artist

Study for *Bodies, Tales, and Landscapes. Progression III*
Courtesy of the artist

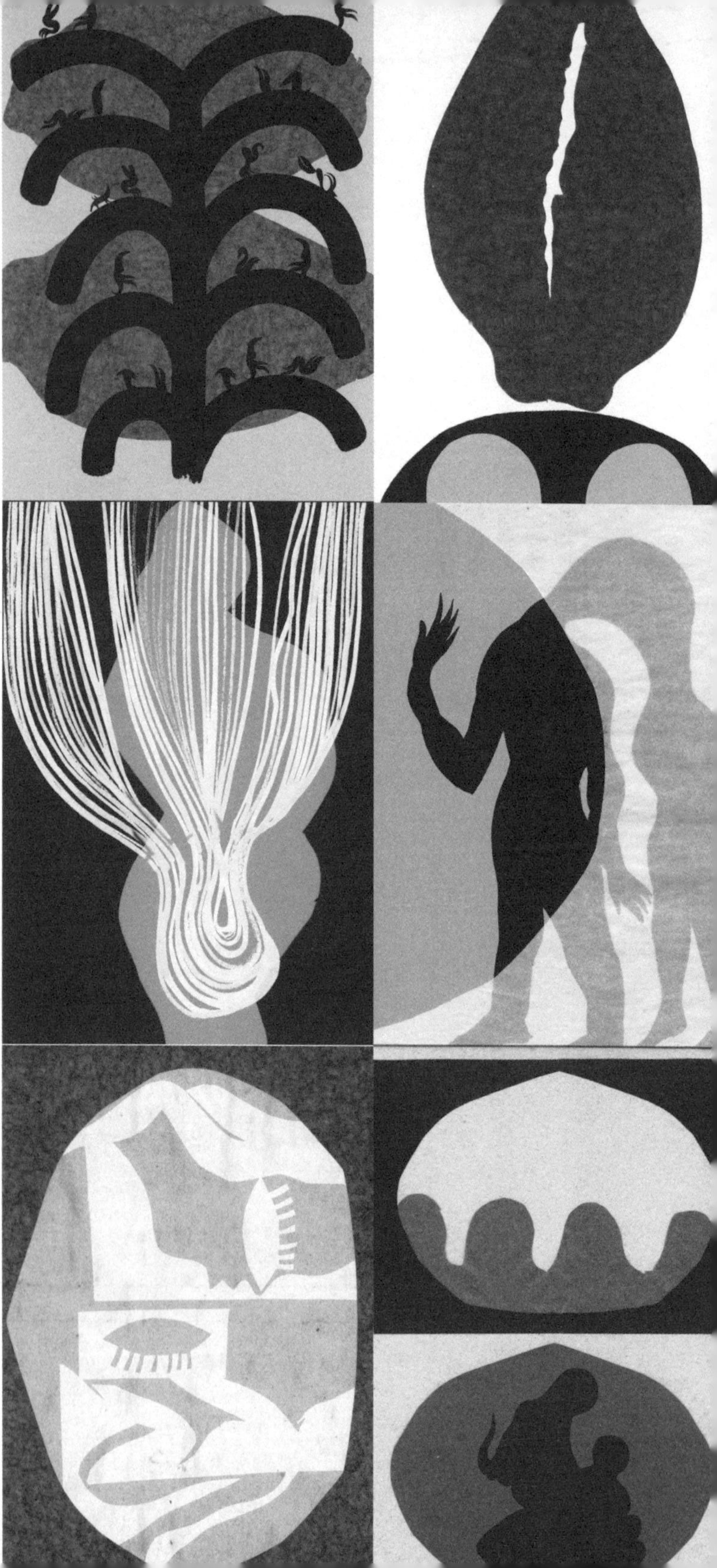

Rubem
Valentim

Farid
Belkahia

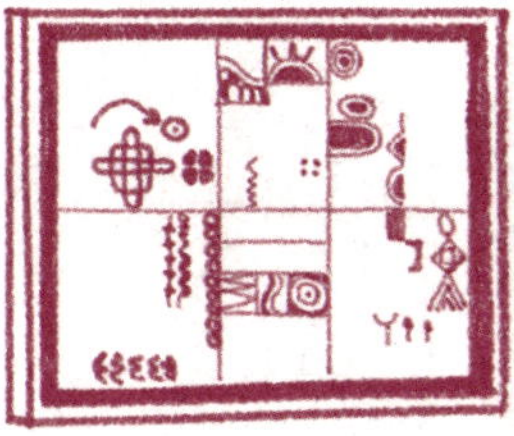

Owusu-Ankomah

1956, Sekondi-Takoradi, Ghana, lives in Bremen, Germany

Owusu-Ankomah

Owusu-Ankomah's practice explores the intersection between symbolism, ontology, and questions of identity throughout a pictorial language centered in the understanding of movement as the defining quality of existence. Drawing from *adinkra* symbols and bodies, much of his work expresses the thoughts, philosophies, values, and histories of Asante people in Ghana. By contemplating the overlapping expansiveness between spiritual, philosophical, and physical realities that get codified in movement and stillness, Owusu-Ankomah blurs the boundaries between past and present, offering an imaginative record of existence. His works *Microcron Begins No.16* and *Microcron Begins No.19* depict adinkra patterns on canvas with superimposed human figures which communicate collective wisdom from the past and propose perspectives for the future. Beyond formalist abstraction, Owusu-Ankomah's art unfolds possibilities to relate to Akan ancient and contemporary Adinkra philosophical symbology, indicating 'universes within universes, within multiverses', as he has described them. Dramatized as figures of being and becoming, the bodies entwined with symbols invite us to a pictorial space that connects us to a system of reflection and meditation. Symbols which convey fondness, alertness, and duty in his work offer trajectories and possibilities for emancipation and exchange. —DMV/PG

Top: *Microcron Begins No.16*. Bottom: *Microcron Begins No.19*.
Photos: Joachim Fliegner

Works in the exhibition:
Microcron Begins No.16 (2013), painting, acrylic on canvas, 180 × 280 cm; *Microcron Begins No.19* (2013), painting, acrylic on canvas, 180 × 280 cm. Courtesy of the artist and October Gallery, London

1934, Marrakesh, Morocco–2014, Marrakesh, Morocco

Farid Belkahia

Farid Belkahia is known for his paintings and leather and metal works influenced by traditional Berber culture and Morocco's architecture. As a modernist artist, who was deeply moved by the independence movements in Africa, he has made decisive contributions to art in the twentieth century through his inclusion of post-colonial perspectives. During the Cold War, he studied painting in Paris and theatre in Prague and when he returned to Morocco in the 1960s, he became director of the Casablanca Ecole des Beaux-Arts and co-founder of the Casablanca School movement. By then Belkahia had consciously distanced himself from the classical tradition of French painting and created a new visual language which placed the symbolism of Moroccan heritage at the centre of his work, while still pointing to his experiences with the minimalist and modernist aesthetic of Eastern and Western Europe. This dialogue is exemplified by *Patchwork Culturel* in which he employs traditional Moroccan techniques and materials, such as henna and animal hides, instead of using western art staples such as canvas and oil paints. His pictorial language is composed of circles, lines, and geometrical forms, mixed with Tifinagh letters, generating a dynamic which breaks with colonial hierarchies and establishes Belkahia as a critical pioneer in questioning and transgressing the colonial legacy of art. —EFB

VG Bild-Kunst, Bonn 2023. Photo: Courtesy of
e Ramzi and Saeda Dalloul Art Foundation, Beirut

Work in the exhibition:
Patchwork Culturel (1979), painting, pigments on skin mounted on panel, 99.5 × 130 cm. Courtesy of The Ramzi and Saeda Dalloul Art Foundation, Beirut

1922, Salvador, Bahia, Brazil–1991,
São Paulo, Brazil

Rubem Valentim

One of the first Afro-Brazilian artists to achieve an international profile, the self-taught painter and sculptor Rubem Valentim brought global attention to the sacred symbology of Candomblé and other Afro-Brazilian spiritist practices brought to Abya Yala by enslaved Yoruba peoples from West and Central Africa. In the *Emblema* series, Valentim appropriates the mid-century turn to abstraction and concretism as his work pools and transmutes the popular aesthetic through various elements of Afro-Atlantic symbolism and diagrams that historically reference the *orishas* (Yoruba spirits). Valentim's visual language thus opposes the avant-gardist claim to newness by sourcing their methods through Brazilian points of reference: the land and people whose culture dominates the Afro-Brazilian coasts of Bahia and those who are often slighted in the larger national discourse. Valentim's work acknowledges Brazil's cultural complexities as he approaches the ancient practice of Candomblé through a mathematical language that questions frameworks of exoticism and places it in conversation with spirit worlds. —SM

Work in the exhibition:
***Emblema V*, 1973, painting, acrylic on canvas, 120 × 73 cm**
Courtesy of Estate Rubem Valentim and Mendes Wood DM, São Paulo, Brussels and New York

Photo: Bruno Leão

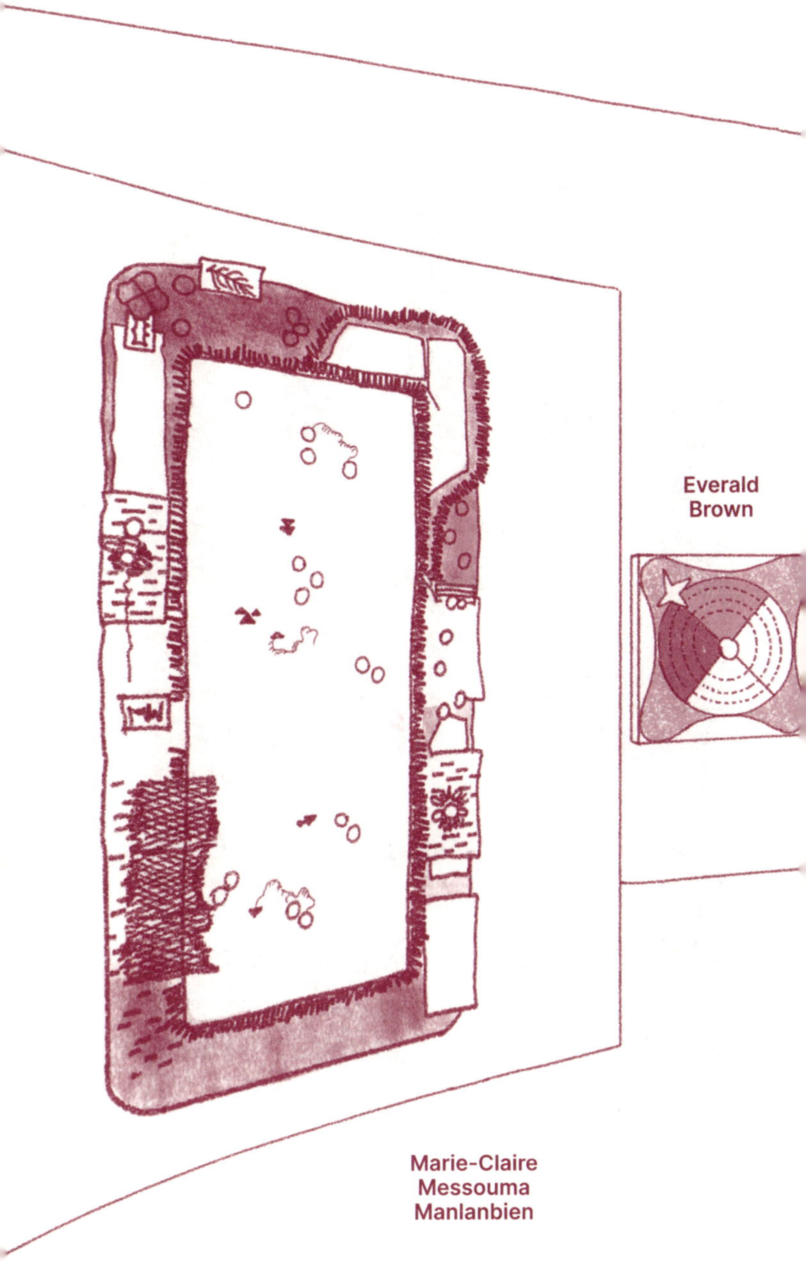
Everald
Brown
Marie-Claire
Messouma
Manlanbien

Abdias
Nascimento
Abdias
Nascimento

1914, Franca, São Paulo–2011,
Rio de Janeiro, Brazil

Abdias Nascimento

Oxunmaré Ascende (Oshumare Rising). Right: *Quilombismo (Exu e Ogum)*. Photos: Miguel Pacheco e Chaves, RCS Arte Digital

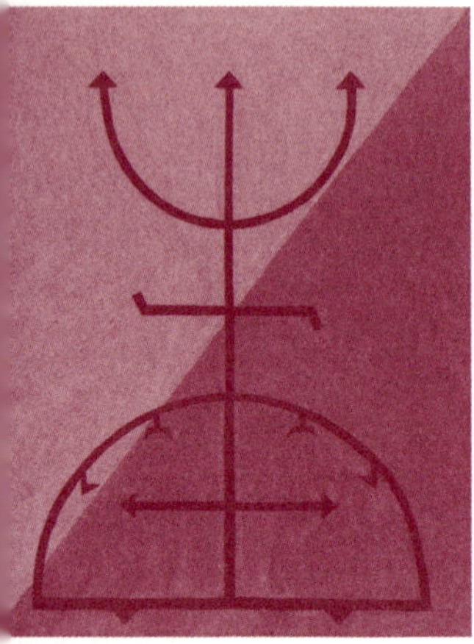

Vorks in the exhibition:
'onto Riscado da Liberdade Sacred Sign for Freedom) (1974), ainting, acrylic on canvas, 202 × 02 cm; *Quilombismo (Exu e Ogum) Kilombism (Eshu and Ogun))* 1980), painting, oil on canvas, 71 56 cm; *Afro Estandarte (African tandard)* (1993), painting, acrylic n canvas, 80 × 50 cm; *Teogonia fro-Brasileira n. 2: Iansã, Obatalá, xum, Oxóssi, Yemanjá, Ogum, ssaim, Xangô, Exu (Afro-Brazilian heogony n. 2: Iansan, Obatala, shun, Oshossi, Yemanja, Ogun, sanyin, Shango, Eshu)* (1972), ainting, acrylic on canvas, 102 × 52 cm; *Baía de Sangue (Luanda) Bay of Blood (Luanda))* (1996), ainting, acrylic on canvas, 80 100 cm; *Oxunmaré Ascende Oshumare Rising)* (1972), painting, crylic on canvas, 152 × 102 cm
ourtesy of Instituto de Pesquisas Estudos Afro-Brasileiros IPEAFRO luseu de Arte Negra

Artist, author, and activist Abdias Nascimento is one of the most crucial figures in the Afro-Brazilian and African worlds. A prolific practitioner from the 1940s onwards, Nascimento jointly developed a pluriversal modernism and a philosophy of *quilombismo*. Working at the intersection of politics and arts, he advocated for racial equality and the affirmation of African epistemologies as knowledges of aesthetic, political, and spiritual worlds that resisted (neo)colonialism. In the Brazilian context, Nascimento contested the myth of 'racial democracy' that denied structural racism within society and embraced the anti-colonial movements of Négritude and Pan-Africanism to vindicate African cultures through global solidarity. Based in Rio de Janeiro, Nascimento founded the Teatro Experimental do Negro (1944), the newspaper *Quilombo* (1948), the Museu de Arte Negra (1950), and the IPEAFRO (1981), among other initiatives. His pictorial works emerged while he was in exile in the US (1968–81) during Brazil's dictatorship. Against the extractivist, formalist, and colonial concepts of 'primitivism', 'pure abstraction', and 'universalism' of western modernism, his paintings are an 'act of love' that express the agency and situated realities of African beings. Encompassed within them are symbols of the *orishas*, the spirits of the Afro-Brazilian Candomblé religion, the adinkra ideograms of West Africa or aphorisms of ancient Egypt, and contemporaneous quilombist struggles, such as the war of independence in Angola (1961–74). —PG

HKW wishes to sincerely thank IPEAFRO / Afro-Brazilian Studies and Research Institute for their collaboration.

As a self-taught artist belonging to the Ethiopian Coptic Orthodox Church, Everald Brown's practice spans sculpture, carving, and painting and is often closely tied to his spiritual values and beliefs as a practising Rastafarian. Brown worked as a carpenter and tried his hand as a musician, both endeavours that were mediated by Rastafarianism and reggae. Consequently, his art referenced older Jamaican cultural movements such as Revivalism and Kumina, which drew upon the rituals of both Christian and West African faiths. In *Mystical Signs*, for example, the artist evokes a compass or a dart board. This circular form is divided into yellow, red, green, and black sections—colours that reference the Jamaican flag (black, green, and gold), the pan-African flag (red, black, and green), as well as the Ethiopian flag (green, yellow, and red). Flanked by four bays of blue, the circle appears to be waterborne, as if floating upon an ocean. Taking this further, the round form can also be read as an island or a ring; a metaphorical take on Rastafarianism or spiritualism as a lifebuoy or a site of refuge, offering orientation, rest, and retreat.
—EOS

Works in the exhibition:
Cotton Duppy Tree **(1994), painting, mixed media on canvas, 82 × 62 cm;** ***Ethiopian Apple*** **(1970), painting, oil on canvas, 63.5 × 90 cm;** ***Mystical Signs*** **(1994), painting, oil on hardboard, 120 × 120 cm;** ***Dove Harp*** **(c. 1973), instrument, metal painted plywood, wood, plastic, H: 64.5 cm;** ***Starry Harp (Instrument for four people)*** **(1986), instrument, metal painted plywood, wood, plastic, H: 73 cm. Courtesy of the National Gallery of Jamaica, Kingston**

1917, Mado District, St. Ann,
Jamaica–2003, New York City, US

Everald Brown

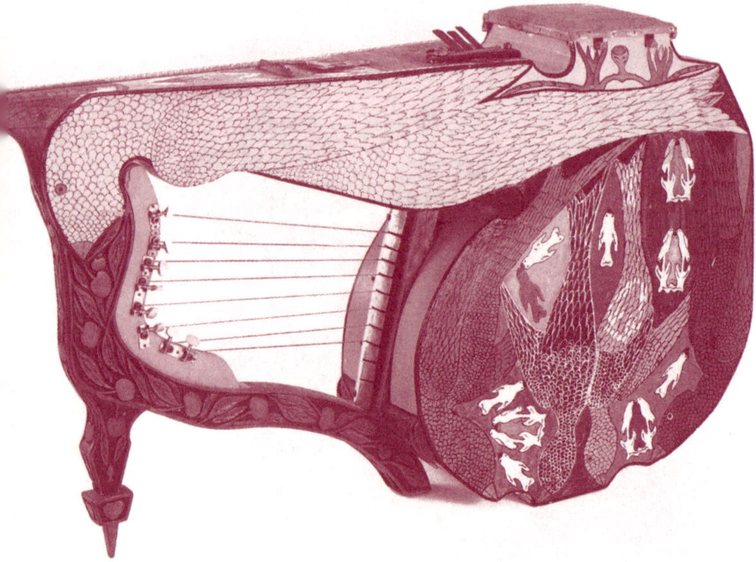

Starry Harp (Instrument for four people). Photo: Courtesy of the National Gallery of Jamaica, Kingston

1990, Paris, France,
lives there

Marie-Claire Messouma Manlanbien

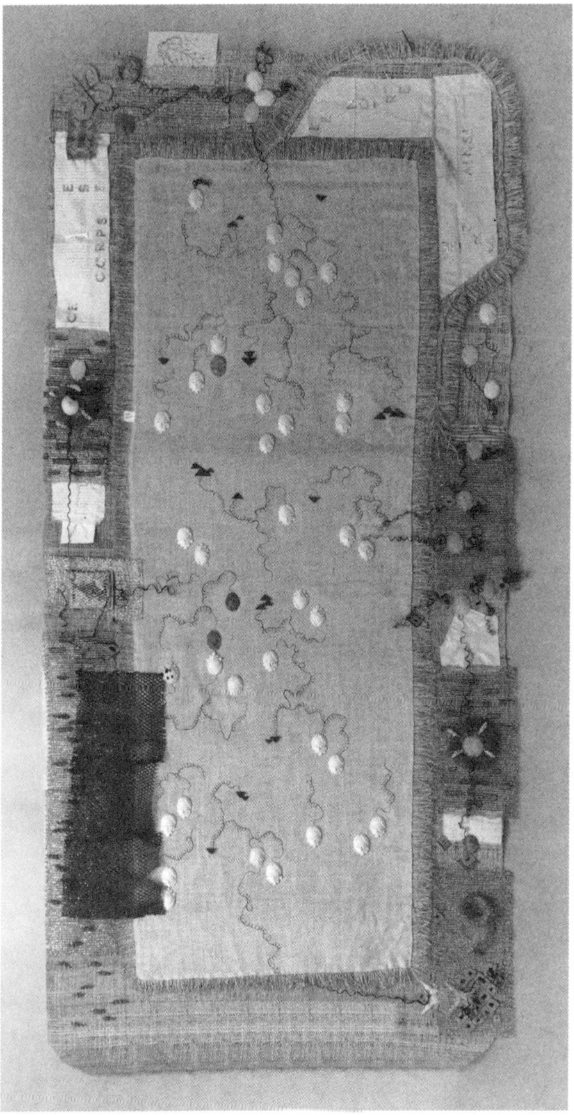

#Map, a series of works that became central to Marie-Claire Messouma Manlanbien's practice, are a combination of cartographies that connect traditional, political, and social threads from the geographies that constructed her identity as an artist. The use of organic materials like hair and raffia fibre refers to a particular sensitivity to the living and breathing aspects of her artistic creations. Emphasizing the notion of the collective body, *#Map* is a non-figurative representation of what cannot be seen but can be caressed and worn, creating a poetic space and experimental field where a non-orchestrated activation takes place once the viewer enters into contact with the work. *#Map—Ce Corps est le nôtre*, the chosen title, pushes the viewer to question whose affirmation it is. Is Messouma Manlanbien calling for a revival of collective memories that haven't been represented enough? Is she rather conveying a message from the living beings that are unseen but heard through the rituals that she portrays in her work? *#Map—Ce Corps est le nôtre* offers a strong foundation to the notions of collectivity and commonality emphasized by Abdias Nascimento in his philosophy of *quilombismo* and throughout the exhibition. —AOW/MHP

Work in the exhibition:
#Map–Ce corps est le nôtre **[This Body is Ours] (2021), jute fibre, hair, scraper, raffia fibre, aluminum, copper, resin, kita, 123 × 257 cm**
Courtesy of Galerie Cécile Fakhoury, Abidjan, Dakar, and Paris

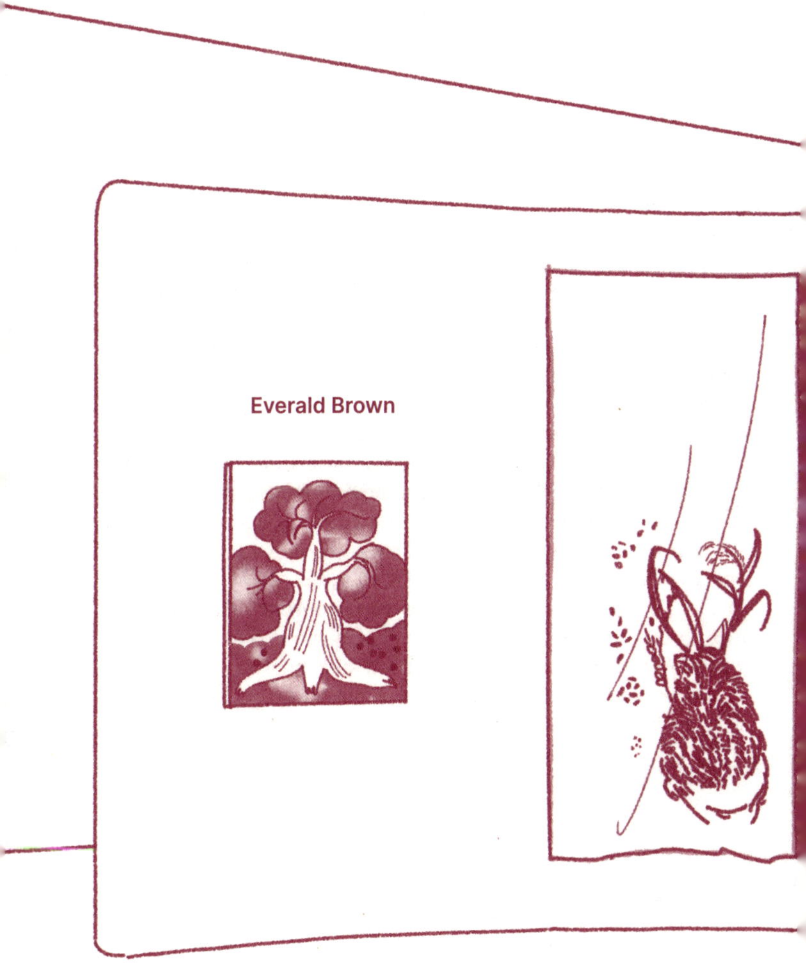

Lizette Nin

Charmaine
Watkiss

1964, London, UK,
lives there

Charmaine Watkiss

To stand Independent and proud I. © VG Bild-Kunst, Bonn 2023
Photo: Courtesy of the artist

Born in London to Jamaican parents, Charmaine Watkiss's work is concerned with remembered stories narrated through strong imaginaries that centre nature and plant-related wisdom from African and Afro-Caribbean traditions. She explores the healing power of her Jamaican matrilineal line which her aunt introduced her to at a young age. In her drawings, she depicts warrior queen figures, whose bodies are adorned with plants believed to hold healing powers that are capable of bringing about peace and social transformation. The use of natural materials like coffee and charcoal is a reminder of 500 years of exploitation and enslavement of African people, who were sent on a journey of no return to produce goods that would form the basis of European wealth. Watkiss has dedicated her practice to tracing African traditions that survived the transatlantic voyage and became the foundation of Caribbean culture. She often uses her own likeness as a reference, depicting herself in an upright and proud posture as if she were a vehicle of communitarian knowledge and experience. The figure of the warrior plant queen stands firm, rooted in traditional beliefs and holding the promise of healing centred in her body, mind, and spirit. —MHP

Works in the exhibition:
***The Seed Sower's Almanack* (2022), painting, coffee, graphite, pencil, carbon pencil, watercolour, 22 ct gold leaf, ink on paper, framed, 162 × 66 cm; *The Warrior's Way: Recalling the lost legacies* (2022), painting, coffee, graphite, pencil, carbon pencil, watercolour, 22 ct shell gold, ink on paper, framed, 86 × 66 cm; *To stand Independent and proud I* (2022), painting, coffee, graphite, pencil, watercolour, 22 ct shell gold, ink on paper, framed, 86 × 66 cm. Courtesy of the artist and Tiwani Contemporary, London and Lagos**

1984, Jimaní, Dominican Republic,
lives in Barcelona, Spain

Lizette Nin

Lizette Nin is a visual artist and researcher whose practice is intersectional, engaging with the deconstruction and reconstruction of Afrocentric histories by creating languages that navigate and thereby negotiate origins, identities, and corporeal existences. Her artistic practice involves the palimpsest: rewriting and retelling the untold and forgotten histories of racialized bodies in a historical continuum. By delicately composing a hybrid image that organically binds braided hair with growing plants, Nin revisits in *Trails* her series of drawings, *Bajar con trenzas*, which renders the locus of Black hair as a weapon of resistance and anti-colonial consciousness. In these drawings, the new image that emerges from the seeds hidden in the braids becomes the carrier of escape routes, a way out of enslavement, a way into the world. In the tradition of marronage as the formation of a community of fugitive enslaved people, *Trails* playfully depicts the tension between roots and routes, between being rooted and having to escape. —AOW

Works in the exhibition:
***Trails* (2021/23), prints, paint on fabric, 120 × 260 cm. Courtesy of the artist**

Top: *En la corona todo crece* (2022), ink on paper
Bottom: *Higuerta para las hebras* (2022), ink on paper
Courtesy of the artist

1961, Kingston, Jamaica, lives
in Port of Spain, Trinidad

Jasmine Thomas-Girvan

Jasmine Thomas-Girvan is known for her aesthetic of assemblages which combine literary, oral, and performative practices with the visual. As Annalee Davis has stated, Thomas-Girvan 'binds varied materials together, connects the logical, linear plane with the supernatural, and links the human interior space with exterior realities.' *The Healing Stream* is an installation that unfolds like a scroll. Drawn on black paper, it centres Rastafari culture and pays homage to *The Royal Parchment Scroll of Black Supremacy* from 1926 by proto-Rastafarian preacher Fitz Balintine Pettersburg. The title *The Healing Stream* stems from a Jamaican folk song that urges: 'Dip dem in the healing stream/ Dip dem deep, but not too deep/ Dip dem to cure bad feelings', reminding the viewer that Black history engages with the power of healing through preached words, whether in song or in service. *The Promised Key*, on the other hand, is a small sculptural work that upholds the 1926 pamphlet under the same name published by Leonard Howell or the 'first Rastafarian' under his Hindu pen name G.G. Maragh. Preaching the history of redemption of Black people through space and time, Howell was later arrested for sedition and became a lifelong target of the colonial government for his activism. —AOW

Works in the exhibition:
The Healing Stream (2022), installation, paper, graphite, acrylic, wood, L: 360 cm (Mrinalini Mukherjee Hall); *The Promised Key* (2023), 7.6 × 7.6 × 10.1 cm, installation, glass, sterling silver, paper (Beatriz Nascimento Hall); *Babylon's Fortune foretold...But what about us?* (2022), installation, transparent film, wood, 22.6 × 29 × 7.5 cm (Beatriz Nascimento Hall). Courtesy of the artist

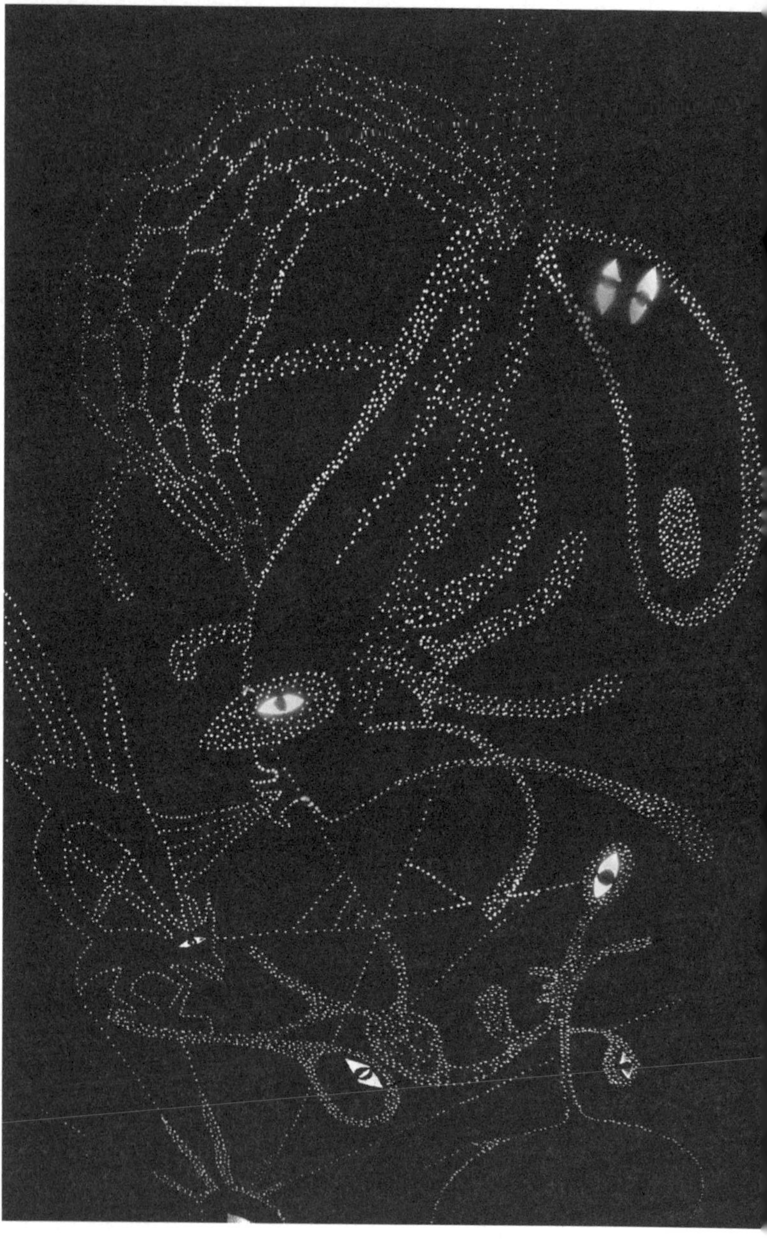

The Healing Stream (2020), detail
Photo: Nathan Patrick

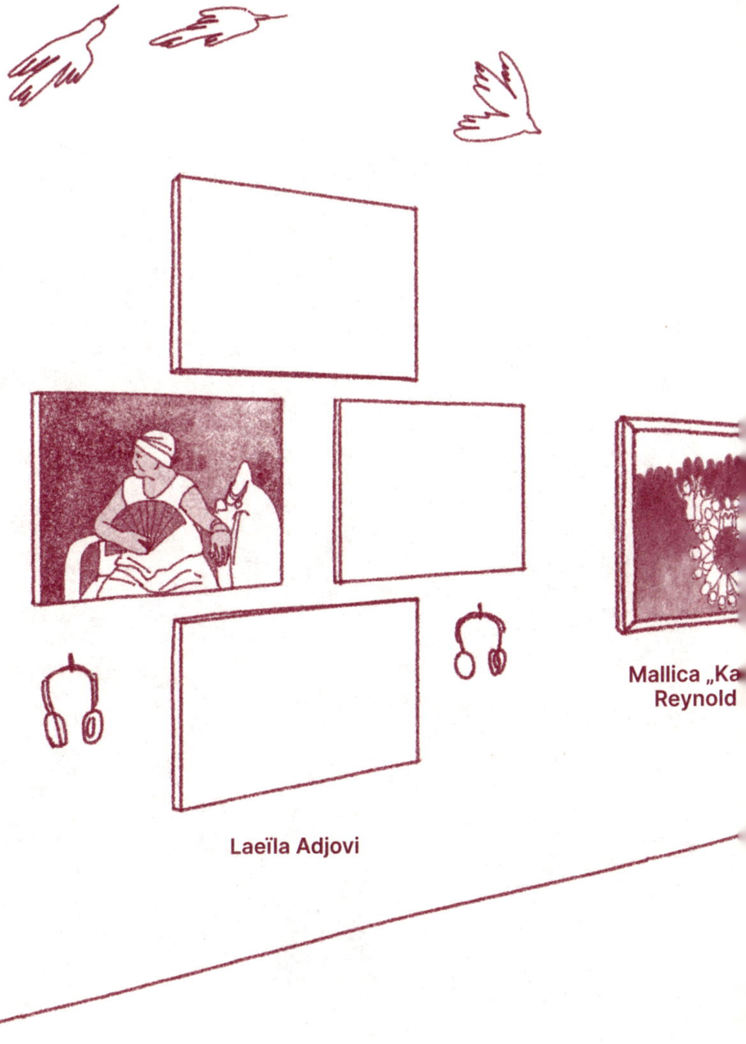

Laeïla Adjovi
Mallica „Ka
Reynold

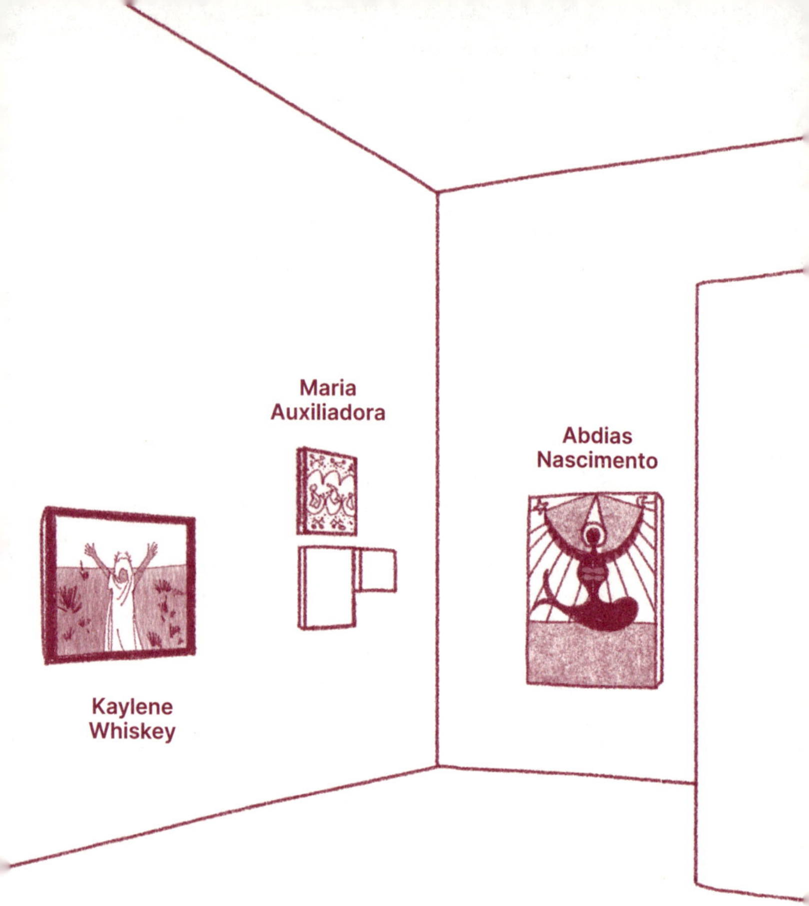
Maria Auxiliadora
Abdias Nascimento
Kaylene Whiskey

1982, Paris, France,
lives in Dakar, Senegal

Laeïla Adjovi

Beninese Laeïla Adjovi is a reporter, photographer, author, and artistic researcher based in Dakar who studied journalism and political science in France before working in India and the Pacific island of New Caledonia. While this background informed her self-taught photographic practice, her artistic approach brings together sound, painting, and drawing, alongside manipulation in the darkroom. In her work, she employs storytelling to interrogate relationships between different social classes, cultures, and worlds. In 2018, Adjovi began the series *The Roads of Yemoja*, parts of which constitute her contribution to *O Quilombismo*. The photographs and sound pieces depict forms of solidarity between peoples, including those of non-African descent. The interdisciplinary project searches for traces of the Yoruba water deity Yemoja, whose traditions are practised by communities on the West African coast, as well as across the Caribbean and South America. The work *El Chino*, for example, shows a religious leader, a descendant of Chinese indentured labourers who embraced Yemoja as a result of the close ties established between Chinese community workers and African people in the Caribbean. Elsewhere in the series, through her exploration of the relationship between Yoruba and Ewe-Fon cultural heritage in Cuba, Adjovi reflects upon disseminated collective memory and cultural hybridization. —EFB

Agramonte, Cuba (2020), from the series *The Roads of Yemoja*

Works in the exhibition:
From the series *The Roads of Yemoja* (2018–ongoing): *El Chino*; *Transatlantic fervor* (photographic triptych), photo and sound installation, printed on photographic paper, laminated on alubond, framed, 80 × 64 cm; *Atunwa*, sound installation, 8' 40"; *Eclat*, sound installation, 7'; *Transe. mission*, sound installation, 6' 50". Courtesy of the artist

1911, Byndloss, Saint Catherine, Jamaica–1989, Kingston, Jamaica

Mallica 'Kapo' Reynolds

With a career beginning in the 1930s, Mallica 'Kapo' Reynolds's work emerged concurrently with his spiritual practice as a revivalist minister and later bishop. His early artworks can be considered records of the visions he experienced during spiritual encounters he had that characterized his travels across Jamaica and his arrival to Trenchtown, Kingston. He faced significant persecution, and some of his early works are said to have been confiscated as evidence of his Obeah spiritual practices. *Kubalee* is one of his later works from an aerial perspective showing a group of people sharing a meal. In a season of bountiful harvest, the meal is set around a circular table, as is the group of people, some of whom emerge from the lush surroundings bringing in more produce. As a document of the various spiritual traditions that Reynolds was engaged in, the meal represents a convivial gathering, a quotidian ceremony, and celebration that anchors various spiritual practices common in the Caribbean. —EOS

Work in the exhibition:
Kubalee **(1972), painting, acrylic on canvas, 76 × 122 cm. Courtesy of the National Gallery of Jamaica, Kingston**

Photo: Donnette Zacca

1976, Mparntwe [Alice Springs], Australia, lives in Indulkana, Australia

Kaylene Whiskey

Kaylene Whiskey is a Yankunytjatjara artist widely known for her portrayal of strong *kungkas* (women in Pitjantjatjara) in her paintings and videos, where they often mingle with global pop icons such as Tina Turner, Dolly Parton, and Cher, while being equally comfortable with superheroes such as Wonder Woman, and the occasional Christian figure. Her short video *Ngura Pukulpa – Happy Place* offers an extensive view of Whiskey's Country, which she reigns through ancestral connections as well as her camp fabulousness. Flying above the vast expanses, at times accompanied by figures born out of her brush and canvas, she dances with this party crew, erupting in joyous pageantry and celebration, and crossing between the borders of country and fantasy. Animals, spirits, stars, and pop stars all celebrate Whiskey, pointing to the complex landscapes of contemporary First Nations narratives. They hail her as an icon, a diva, and a model of strength and power for women of many worlds who weren't always the centre and the voice of the story. Fun is thus elevated as the highest form of political affirmation of presence and vibrancy by the artist and her community. —CC

Work in the exhibition:
Ngura Pukulpa – Happy Place
(2021), video, 8' 07"
Courtesy of the artist

Ngura Pukulpa – Happy Place (2021), production stills. © VG Bild-Kunst, Bonn 2023. Photos: Max Mackinnon

1935, Campo Belo, Minas Gerais, Brazil–1974, São Paulo, Brazil

Maria Auxiliadora

In the works *Samba* and the untitled agricultural scenes, the self-taught artist Maria Auxiliadora reminds us of the feminist call that the personal is political. Her art depicts scenes of domestic and rural life, of Afro-Brazilian religions, dance, carnivals, and quotidian scenes of festivities and popular culture. Born into a poor, working class home with a strong Afro-Brazilian tradition and artistic tendencies amongst many family members, Auxiliadora began experimenting with different practices early on and continued producing art in parallel to being a domestic worker—work she took on to help sustain her family at the age of twelve. Her later work as an embroiderer in a factory in the Brás neighbourhood of São Paulo found echoes in her practice as she settled on painting, but also continuously added texture and dimension to the pieces, often including her own hair. Auxiliadora's international recognition has come only post-mortem, but her work is now considered a political intervention that reformulates the representation of non-hegemonic cultures and the everyday life and bodies that inhabit them. —SM

Works in the exhibition:
Samba **(1969), painting, mixed media on canvas, 49.7 × 64.6 cm. Courtesy of Musée d'Art Naïf et des Arts Singuliers, Laval; *Untitled* (1972), painting, mixed media on canvas, 19 × 26 cm; *Untitled* (1974), painting, gouache on cardboard glued to eucatex, 50.5 × 67 cm. Courtesy of Estate Maria Auxiliadora and Mendes Wood DM, São Paulo, Brussels, and New York**

Samba. Photo: Courtesy of Musée d'Art Naïf et des Arts Singuliers, Laval

Untitled (1974). Photo: Bruno Leão

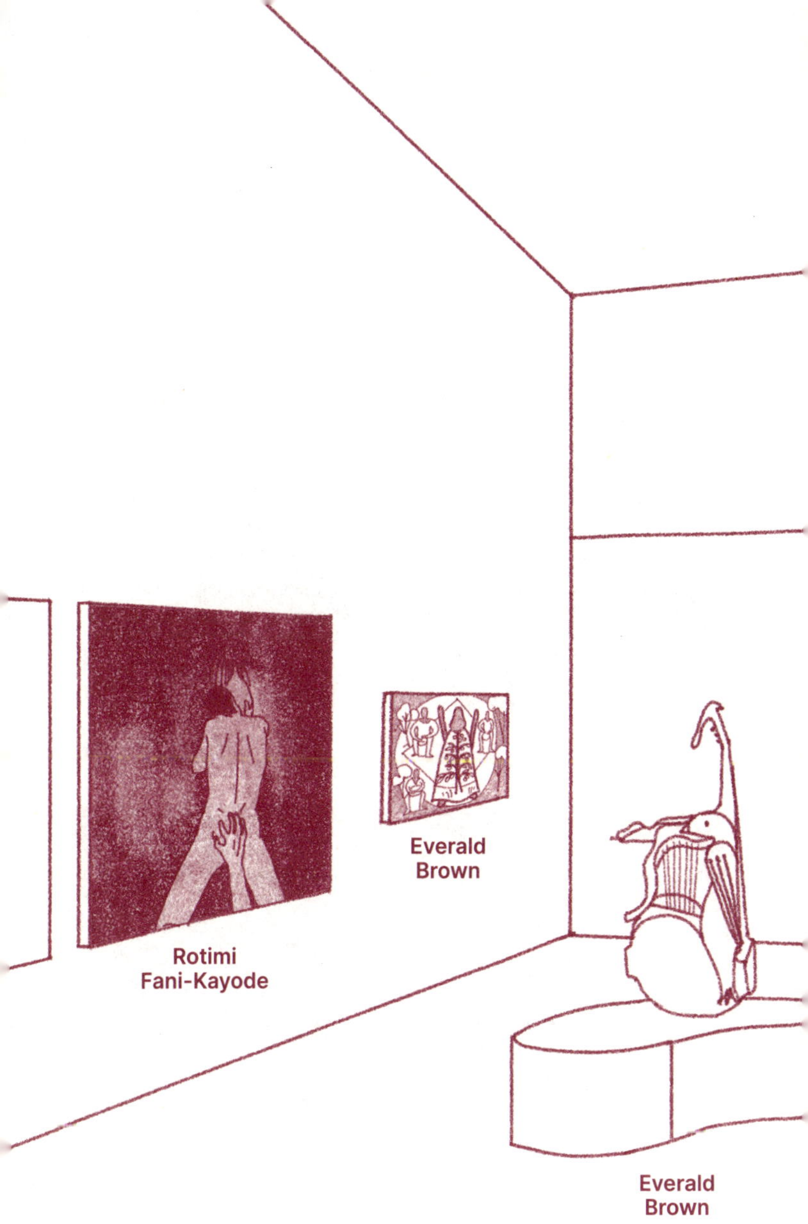
Rotimi
Fani-Kayode
Everald
Brown
Everald
Brown

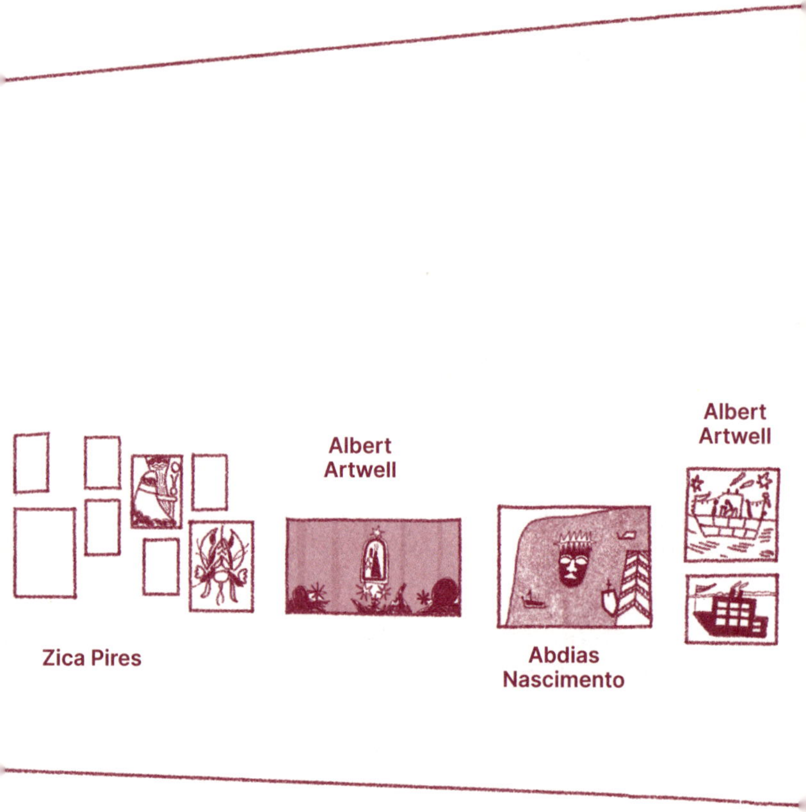
Albert
Artwell
Albert
Artwell
Zica Pires
Abdias
Nascimento

1955, Ile-Ife, Nigeria–1989,
London, UK

Rotimi Fani-Kayode

A seminal figure in Black British photography circles in the 1980s, Rotimi Fani-Kayode's practice was informed by an unflinching interrogation of the intersections between queerness, spirituality, and the African masculinized body. Produced in 1987, *Sonponnoi* shows the almost naked torso and thighs of a young Black man. Black, white, and pink spots are painted on the figure's body, whose hands hold five candles—each lit with glowing tongues of fire—between his thighs. Sculptural representations of the Yoruba god of earth and disease, Ṣọ̀pọ̀na, referenced by the work's title, often depict him as covered with coloured spots. Yet Ṣọ̀pọ̀na is also the god of healing in Yoruba mythology—emphasizing the nuance between and around binaries such as healthy/diseased. One of Fani-Kayode's last works *Every Moment Counts* shows the naked back of a young Black man, who is crunched forward in a pose that makes him particularly vulnerable to the photographer's—and the viewer's—gaze. A hand, emerging from between his legs, grabs his buttocks from below, heightening the tension of the composition. A white mask, evoking the one plague doctors are said to have worn in the seventeenth century is flanked by thin strands of black hair. The work highlights the spectral threat that HIV posed to queer communities in the 1980s, and the disproportionate exposure Black queer people faced due to both stigma and racism in the health sector and beyond. Fani-Kayode's bold subversion of Yoruba symbols and systems of representation continue to signal horizons of freedom and resistance for queer Africans today. —EOS

Works in the exhibition:
Every Moment Counts (1989), photography, 120 × 120 cm
Untitled (1987–88), photography, 120 × 120 cm
Untitled (1987–88), photography, 120 × 120 cm
Courtesy of The Walther Collection, Neu-Ulm

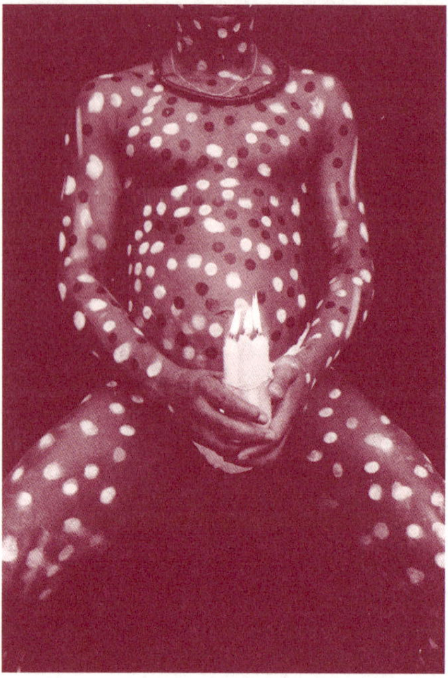

Sonponnoi (1987) © Rotimi Fani-Kayode
Courtesy of Autograph, London

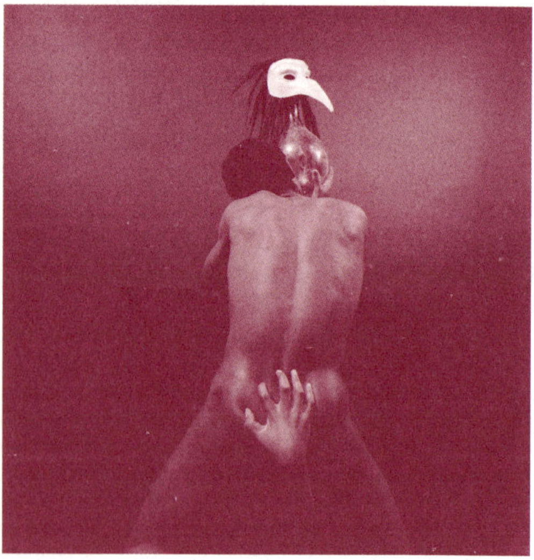

Every Moment Counts (Ecstatic Antibodies) (1989)
© Rotimi Fani-Kayode, Courtesy Autograph, London

1994, quilombo Santa Rosa dos Pretos, Itapecuru-Mirim, Maranhão, Pindorama, Brazil, has lived in the quilombo Santa Rosa dos Pretos for 347 years and also, only since 1994

Zica Pires

Zica Pires is an artist and activist invested in the fight against water privatization, bringing forth international awareness and lending her voice to the ¡Água para os povos! (water for the poor!) campaign across social media platforms. Born in the *quilombo* Santa Rosa dos Pretos de Itapecuru-Mirim, a site founded by Black people revolting against their enslavement who were brought to plantations from Guinea Bissau, the young artist values the roots and cultures of the quilombos. In addition, she is engaged in teaching the history and culture of African and Indigenous people in primary and secondary education. Her art is a reflection of her pedagogical and activist practices, inseparable from her quilombo roots and their histories of struggle for Black liberation. The selection of illustrations, which carry titles such as *Cidade Possivel* (Possible City), depict goddesses or thematize the intertwining of nature and human infrastructure, proposing a future that unfolds in harmony with human and non-human life. —SM

Works in the exhibition:
Lord (2020), painting, ballpoint pen, coloured pencil on paper, 21 × 29.7 cm; *Dambirãn* (2022), painting, graphite, india ink, fabric paint, acryl on canvas, 30 × 23 cm; *Guinça* [Orientation] (2022), painting, acryl, beads, feather on canvas, 30 × 23 cm; *Cidade Possível* [Possible City] (2021), painting, ballpoint pen on paper, 21 × 29.7 cm; *Velho do alto do mundo* [Old man from the top of the world] (2023), painting, crayons on paper, 21 × 29.7 cm; *Mensageiro* [Messenger] (2023), painting, coloured pencils on paper, 21 × 29.7 cm; *Mãe d'água* [Mother of water] (2023), painting, coloured pencils on paper, 21 × 29.7 cm; *Caminho de Narrativas Quilombolas* [Quilombo narrative trail] (2023), drawing, graphite on paper, 21 × 29.7 cm; *Zandia Ayala* (2023), drawing, graphite on paper, 60 × 30 cm; *Cigarra* [Cicada] (2023), painting, watercolour on paper, 29.7 × 42 cm; *Semente* [Seed] (2023), painting, watercolour on paper, 29.7 × 42 cm. Courtesy of the artist

Cidade Possível. Photo: Courtesy of the artist

1942, Catadupa, St. James, Jamaica–2018, St. James, Jamaica

Albert Artwell

Considered one of the founders of the Jamaican intuitive movement, Albert Artwell is known for his distinctive flat-painted and illustrative style. Artwell typically uses humour in his depiction of well-known scenes from the Bible, introducing moments of situational comedy that are often absent from biblical descriptions. His work has often been attributed to the art brut movement, a tendency that can overlook the artist's eye for social criticism. An untitled painting by Artwell, often referred to as *Black Star Liner*, shows a black ship preparing to set sail, presumably back to Africa. The passengers sit in comical seriousness in readiness for their 'return' trip, a cheeky visual reference to the infamous early twentieth-century Back to Africa campaign aimed at African Americans initiated by Jamaican Black nationalist Marcus Garvey. The campaign was a failure because Garvey ignored the agency of his constituents, most of whom had no interest to travel to a distant and unfamiliar promised land but were rather invested in establishing free societies where they were. —EOS

Works in the exhibition:
Judgement Day (1979), painting, oil on hardboard, 60 × 116 cm. Courtesy of the David Boxer/Onyx Foundation; *Untitled* (Red, Green and Gold Boat) (n.d.), painting, acrylic on hardboard, 62 × 62 cm. Courtesy of Herman Van Aesbroek; *Untitled* (Black Star Liner) (n.d.), painting, acrylic on canvas, 48 × 64 cm. Courtesy of Josef Forstmayr

Judgement Day. Photo: Courtesy of the National Gallery of Jamaica, Kingston

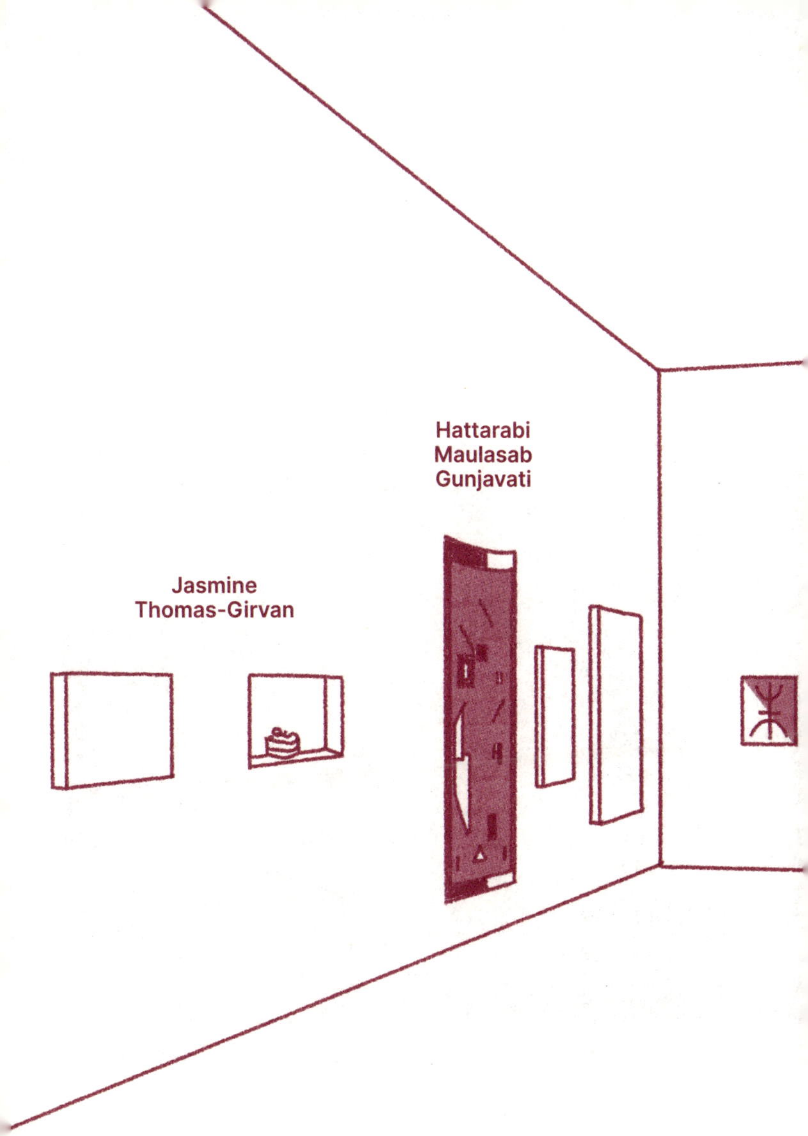
Hattarabi
Maulasab
Gunjavati
Jasmine
Thomas-Girvan

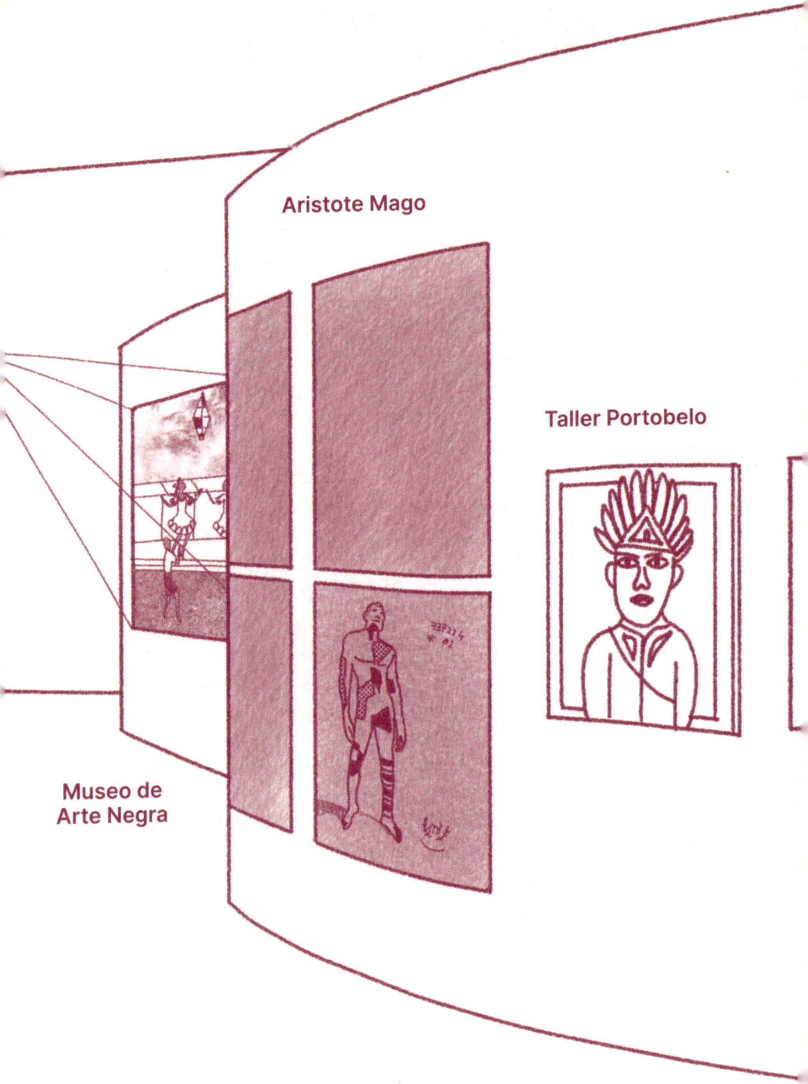

snowfuks
audio work

Taller Portobelo

'Know who you are before someone tells you' is a popular adage among the Wolof people of the Senegambia region of West Africa from whom the Congos of Portobelo, Panama, are descended. It is also the inspiration for the paintings by the members of Taller Portobelo. In 1995, Virgilio 'Yaneca' Esquina, a leading member of the community, together with photographer Sandra Eleta and artist, cultural investigator, and educator Arturo Lindsay, formed the painting workshop where Arte Congo, a new and unique Afro-Panamanian visual arts movement was born. Congos trace their lineage to *cimarrones* (maroons), self-liberated Africans in Panama. Pushing against the erasure through enslavement of African identity, memories, and culture, they continue their forebears' resistance through art, music, dance, language, fashion, food, street performances, fortified villages or *palenques*, and Carnival. Taller Portobelo's contribution to *O Quilombismo* manifests in the plentitude of the depictions of their indelible identity, including the sovereign ruler of their matriarchal society queen María Merced (*María Merced*); an herbal healer (*Hiervatero)*; a king who blends with the tropical landscape (*Rey Guacamayo*); and the resilience of women of colour (as proclaimed in *Judimingue nunko modidá*). Through their practice, Taller Portobelo honour and celebrate this lineage and the ethos of egalitarianism, communitarianism, and a bond with ancestrality and the environment which are at the heart of *quilombismo*. —RC/A

Top: Ariel 'Pajarito' Jiménez, *King Guacamayo*
Bottom: Gustavo Esquina de la Espada, *María Merced*
Photos: Aurora Fierro Eleta

Works in the exhibition: *Know who you are before someone tells you* (2023), paintings of various artists: Gustavo Esquina de la Espada, *María Merced* (2022), painting, acrylic, pieces of broken mirrors on canvas, 70 × 60 cm; Virgilio 'Yaneca' Esquina, *Hiervatero* (2013), painting, acrylic, pieces of broken mirrors on canvas, 78 × 83 cm; Ariel 'Pajarito' Jiménez, *King Guacamayo* (2009), acrylic with pieces of broken mirrors on canvas, 112 × 100 cm; Manuel Tatu Golden, *Judimingue nunko modidá* [Cimarrones never die] (2019), painting, acrylic paint, feathers, shells, seeds, pieces of broken mirrors on canvas, 70 × 60 cm. Courtesy of the artists

1988, Kinshasa, Congo,
lives there

Aristote Mago

Born in Kinshasa, one of the most vibrant cities of the African continent, Aristote Mago, like many other Kinois, has been strongly influenced by the culture of *débrouillardise*—a term that describes creativity and innovation as acts of survival in a fast-evolving city. Mago has developed a practice that layers histories and memories against urgent sociopolitical questions. His technique of recuperation and use of found materials follows a long tradition of art making that emerged in the 1960s in both western and central parts of the African continent. Such an approach was not only a reaction to the lack of available materials used elsewhere in modern artistic practice but also a way of countering the ever-growing consumerist dimensions of art making. Sacks made from jute, a natural fibre, as well as those made of polypropylene are Mago's canvases of choice. Both materials hold a long history of trade and transportation of mass-produced goods such as coffee, bananas, yams, charcoal, and sugar, among others. Through superimposed stitching, the artist depicts scenes of everyday life, centring social and political themes such as land exploitation and the climate crisis, sexuality and queerness, and democracy and free expression. —MHP

Commissioned by Haus der Kulturen der Welt (HKW), co-produced by Aristote Mago and HKW, 2023.

Works in the exhibition:
***Entre Coupe* (2023), painting, mixed media collage synthetic cotton thread, lace on jute canvas, 199 × 150 cm; *Elombe* (2023), painting, mixed media collage synthetic cotton thread, lace on jute canvas, 199 × 150 cm; *Empereur* (2023), painting, mixed media collage synthetic cotton thread, lace on jute canvas, 150 × 149 cm; *Untitled* (2023), painting, mixed media collage, synthetic cotton thread, lace on jute canvas, 150 × 149 cm. Courtesy of the artist**

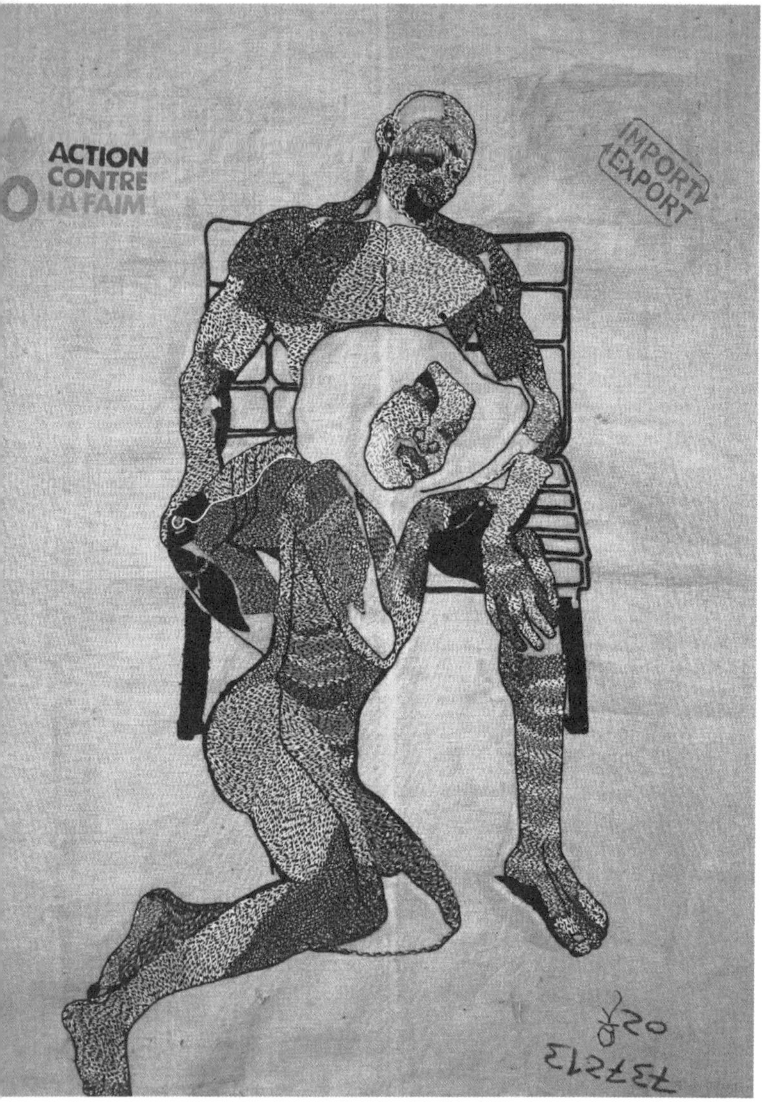

Entre Coupe © VG Bild-Kunst, Bonn 2023. Photo: kin artstudio

Hattarabi Maulasab Gunjavati

The Siddi communities across the western coast of India trace their origins from the eastern regions of the African continent, arriving eastwards over the past millennium at various times and in various circumstances: as merchants on the Somali-Indian coastal trade routes (superseded in later centuries by the Swahili-Indian route), as sailors, mercenaries, aristocrats, and as people who were enslaved. The Siddi legacy in India includes royal houses of Bengal, Ahmadnagar, or Janjira, among many other political and military figures. Several Siddi communities thrive today in India, having established casteless and more egalitarian societies than the surrounding mainstream social structures in the country. Women from Siddi communities have developed a quilting textile practice, one that is continuously evolving and morphing, ever refining a stunning language of vibrant abstraction part of no other art historical genealogy. While the pieces are reminiscent of several quilting practices and artists from different Afro-diasporic communities in the Americas, the Siddi quilts are artistic languages developed locally, with various aesthetic and protective strategies, such as the patterns at the corners of the quilt that are meant to function as amulets and forms of ensuring safety. —CC

Quilts by Bastin Santan Diggekar, Shakirambi Ganishab Tattongi, Bibijan Babushab Gunjavathi, Badimabi Gafarsab Ugrani, and Saidambi Imamasab Naik on display in the Mrinalini Mukherjee Hall, see p. 96.

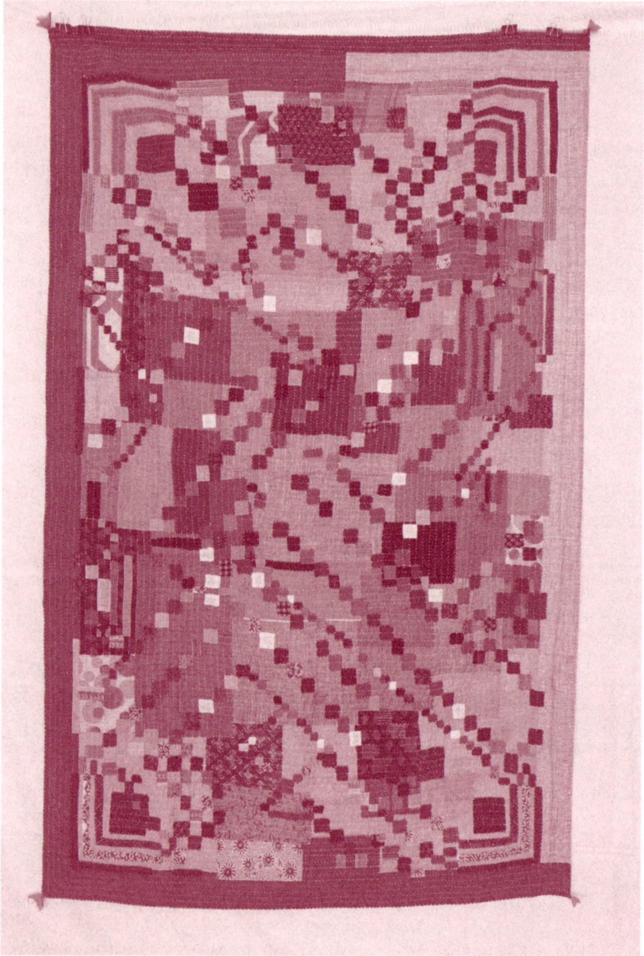

Photo: Anitha N Reddy

Work in the exhibition:
Untitled (2023), textile, hand-stitched siddi kavand (African-Indian quilt) with embroidery, 229 × 280 cm

Museu de Arte Negra

The Museu de Arte Negra (MAN) was founded in 1950 in Rio de Janeiro by the Teatro Experimental do Negro (TEN), directed by Abdias Nascimento. The MAN emerged from the first Congresso do Negro Brasileiro (First Congress of Brazilian Blacks), as a museological model to contest racism and epistemic violence by valuing the art and culture of people of African descent. As with other practices that bring life to the philosophy of *quilombismo*, MAN challenged colonial modern art structures, opening space to artists that have been ignored or whose art has been reduced to ethnographic artefacts. It denounced the looting of African art by western museums, and discussed how to liberate artists from the prejudices inherent within discourses around the 'primitives' or the 'naïve', thus placing African art on an equal footing with modern art. In 1955, it organized the Cristo Negro (Black Christ) competition, in which more than one hundred artists participated, reappropriating the 'alienating aesthetic standards of whiteness'. MAN's activities were interrupted when Nascimento went into exile in 1968 due to the repression of the dictatorship. Since 1981, its collection of some five hundred works has been housed at IPEAFRO, founded by Nascimento upon his return to Rio de Janeiro to insist on the quilombist agenda of cultural affirmation. —PG

HKW wishes to sincerely thank IPEAFRO / Afro-Brazilian Studies and Research Institute for their collaboration.

Selection of artworks from the collection:
Digital slideshow (2023)
Courtesy of Instituto de Pesquisas e Estudos Afro-Brasileiros (IPEAFRO), Rio de Janeiro

Top: Heitor dos Prazeres, *Crianças com balão* [Children with balloons] (1965), oil on canvas. Bottom: Januário, *Belãmin, menina* [Belãmin, girl] (1982), acrylic on canvas

2001, São Paulo, Brazil, lives in
Diamantina, Minas Gerais, Brazil

snowfuks

Work in the exhibition:
Outros Navios (2023), 5', music composition as soundscape in the exhibition space
Produced and performed by snowfuks
Mix/master/guitar: Pedro Henrique da Silva Lima
Poetry/lyrics: Eustáquio Neves
Courtesy of the artists

Outros Navios

Braços tempestuosos,
profundos, atlânticos,
abraçam me liquídos em seu sal,
em torrente veias,
em silencio que atormenta
e congela o tempo
em infinita noite.
Desesperadamente,
preciso romper
a cortina turva que separa
minha mente da razão,
estou a poucos passos do meu segundo inferno
e o primeiro ainda arde em minha carne
estou a um disparo de toda minha crença

A incerteza é a droga que me consome aos poucos
quanto mais incerteza mais entorpece a mente
mas o mar não tem limites, parece.
Arde ainda esse inferno, agora por toda mente
e os sonhos caem em cinzas gris, um a um.
Estou a um disparo de toda minha crença

Ha uma vertigem de cetim sob os pés
na geografia imprecisa.
Um nome que insisto em chamar
trás, uma paz breve e um delírio febril
de seus sussurros colados em meu rosto
e assim me mantenho de pé
quando estou a um disparo de toda minha crença

Esse ópio, o poder,
quer tomar minhas forças,
meus olhos,
meu sexo,
minha mente,
meu corpo, em fim.
Pés que já quase desaprenderam andar
recusam tombar meu corpo sobre essa cova rasa.
quando ainda estou a quase um disparo da minha
crença

Gunta Stölzl Foyer

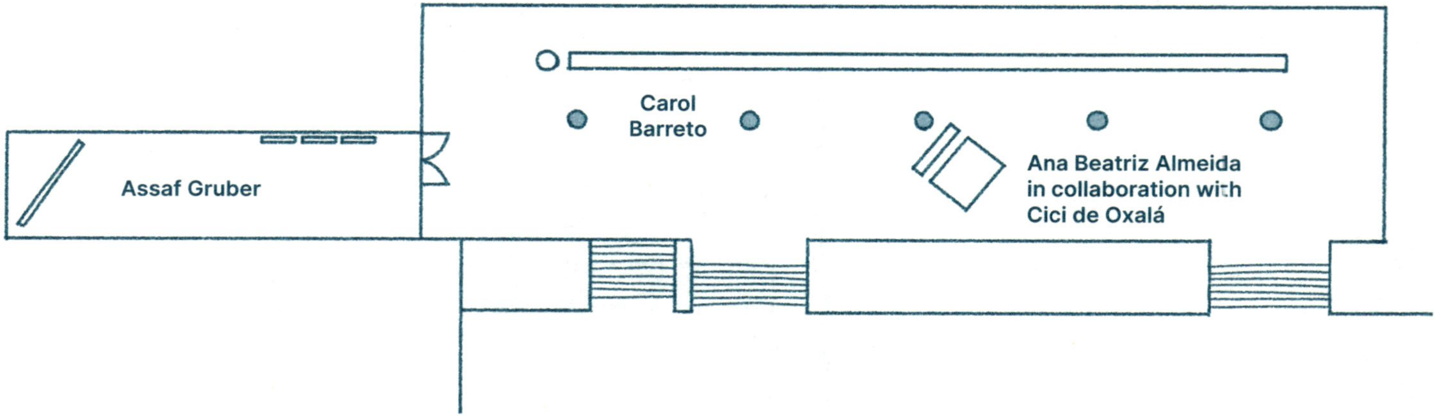
Carol
Barreto
Assaf Gruber
Ana Beatriz Almeida
in collaboration with
Cici de Oxalá

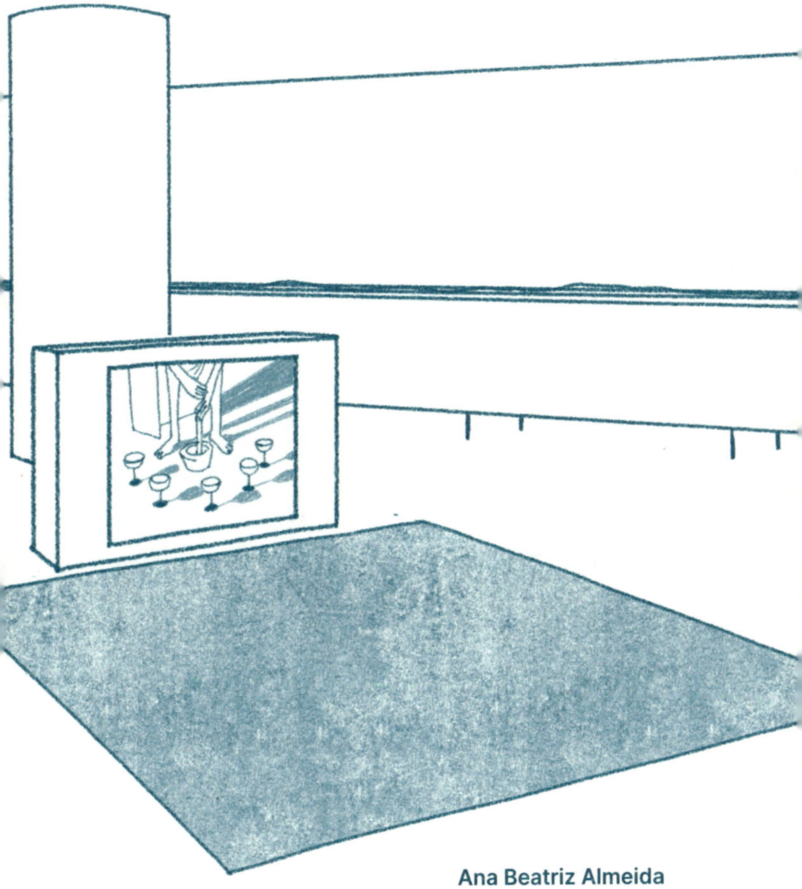

Ana Beatriz Almeida
in collaboration with
Cici de Oxalá

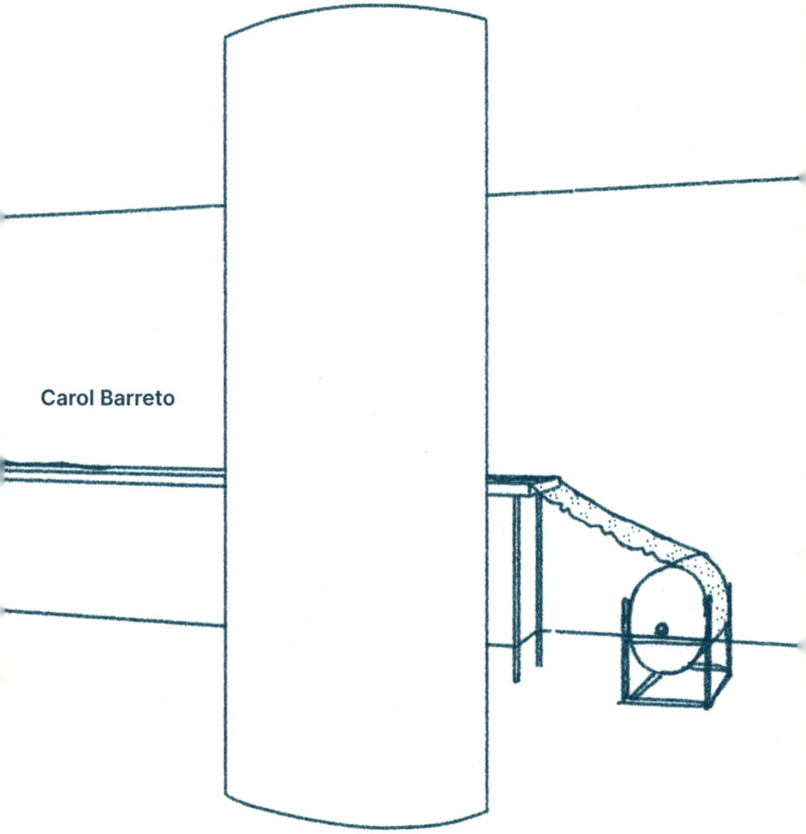

Carol Barreto

1980, Santo Amaro, Bahia, Brazil,
lives in Salvador, Bahia, Brazil

Carol Barreto

Carol Barreto unveils and expands the empowerment and communitarian narratives woven into the making and wearing of fabrics and garments by women from the *quilombos* of Northeast Brazil. A visual artist, university professor, and designer, through her work on *ModAtivismo*, Barreto explores the links between fashion and feminist and anti-racist activism, advocating also for conscious consumption and non-exploitative participation. Barreto's collections such as *VOZES* [Voices] (2015–17) have prompted debates on national and international catwalks not only about the legacies of colonialism but also the resistance of the quilombos of Recôncavo Baiano. The collection *Asè* [life force] (2016–22), inspired by oral, cultural, and religious practices that form an imaginary of return and ancestral connection to Africa, honouring the history of Blackness in Brazil, is the base for her installation *Omi*. A sculptural dress emerges from a long train, reminiscent of a tablecloth, covering forty metres of HKW's cloakroom desk. It is made from different family garments, such as the artist's christening gown and her Yarogba costume from the Candomblé Nação Ketu, joined with pieces of different decorative techniques. The dress is accompanied by a soundscape, composed by Laila Rosa, of waves at Ilha de Maré and the clicking of bobbins of the *quilombola* women with whom she collaborates. —A

Commissioned by Haus der Kulturen der Welt (HKW), co-produced by Carol Barreto and HKW, 2023.

Retrato de Família, photographic series.
Photos: Roque Boa Morte

Works in the exhibition:
Omi [Grandma] (2021–23), installation, fabric, cotton thread, garments, bobbin lace, renaissance lace, fillet lace, fuxico, textile waste, handmade textiles, tablecloth consisting of sixteen pieces of different lace: 260 × 40 cm each, historical pieces of clothing: dimensions vary, and one lace cushion: c. 30 × 45 cm; *Retrato de Família* [Family Portrait] (2021), photography printed on canvas, 138 × 92 cm, photographer: Roque Boa Morte
Courtesy of the artist

1987, Niteroi, Brazil, lives in London, UK

Ana Beatriz Almeida in collaboration with Cici de Oxalá

1939, Rio de Janeiro, Brazil, lives in Salvador, Brazil

Ana Beatriz Almeida is a visual artist and storyteller whose work focuses on African traditions and their connections to the African diaspora throughout history. She has developed a series of rites to honour those who did not survive the transatlantic trade of enslaved people but remain alive in spirit. Focusing on memory, the meaning of life and death, as well as the infinity that resides between both, in this short film Almeida invites the *griot* Cici de Oxalá to narrate the creation of the world. The figure of the griot has a very crucial symbolism within African traditions as holders of collective memory who bind communities together through a tireless transmission of the values of ancestrality and spiritual belief. In Senegalese Wolof traditions, the physical presence of griots after death used to be prolonged by burying their bodies inside the trunks of baobab trees. This, it was believed, would allow the tree to be infused with their knowledge so it would remain close for centuries afterwards. In a strong and poetic gesture, de Oxalá calls for a reconnection to nature by evoking the very first act of creation that brought about the world. —MHP

Photo: Shai Andrade

Work in the exhibition:
Griot narrative on the creation of the world (2022), video, 1' 44"
Courtesy of the artist and Shai Andrade

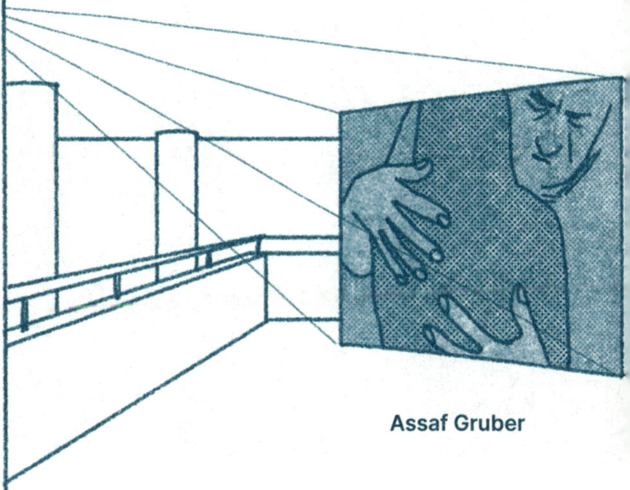

Assaf Gruber

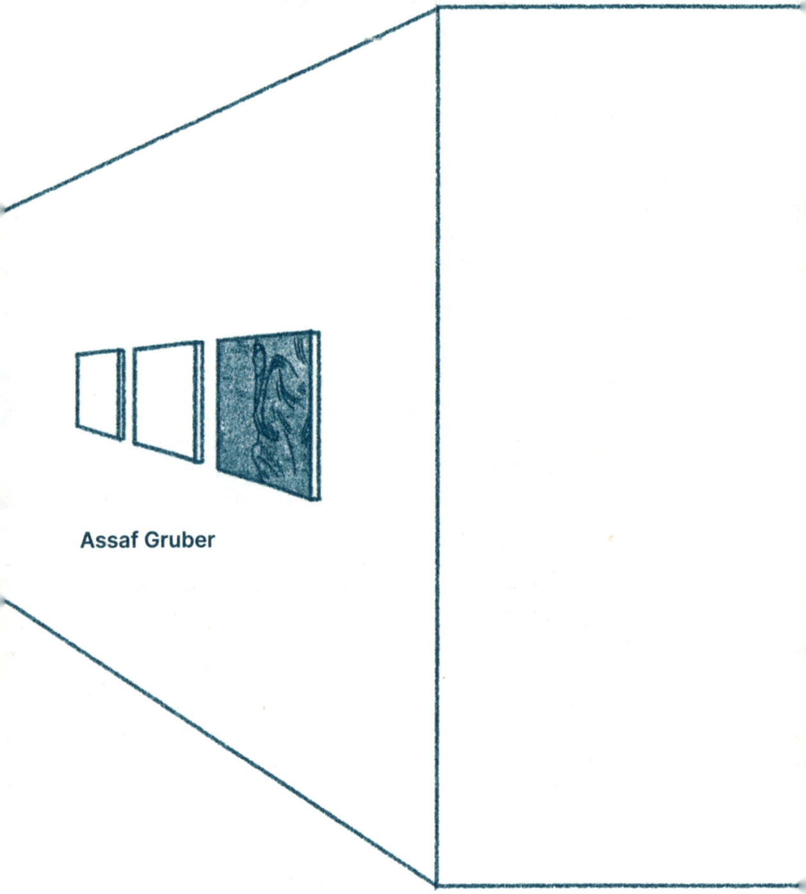

Assaf Gruber

1980, Jerusalem

Assaf Gruber

Never Come Back is a dark archaeological immersion into the conscience and memory of European cultural structures, represented here by an art museum, specifically Graz's Neue Galerie. A naked accordion player wanders through the museum's storage area, pulling out mediocre yet evocative paintings depicting European folkloric scenes, as well as landscapes sometimes populated with animals. The paintings sit on an uncomfortable edge between the pastoral and a certain type of imagery abused by National Socialism. The accordion player seems to be seeking inspiration from the paintings, which he eventually finds; the unrecognizable tunes he tentatively plays throughout the first part of the film eventually come together as a rendition of 'Voyage, Voyage', the oldie-but-goldie pan-European *schlager* of a few decades past. Its deeply disturbing lyrics—which one may have missed—are then revealed, overlaid on scenes and close-ups of the paintings. These are made by artists who were indeed Nazi enthusiasts, yet their work is still kept in the vaults of museums. The song's lyrics convey a cringe exoticism and desire to consume and possess a world as imagined by an imperial European mind. The film's title is also part of the lyrics, while uncannily alluding to the ghosts of Nazism and colonialism that still haunt Europe. Alongside the video, an uncanny series of photographs, *The Conspicuous Parts,* depicts coral in seemingly-natural landscapes, which are in fact dioramas preserved in formaldehyde. These are a remnant of another unexpected colonial adventure involving an expedition to Cuba by the German Democratic Republic in the 1960s, during which six tonnes of coral were extracted. —CC

Works in the exhibition:
***Never Come Back* (2022), video installation;**
***The Conspicuous Parts* (2018),**
C-Prints, dimensions vary
Courtesy of the artist

Video stills

Ceija Stojka Foyer, Miriam Makeba Auditorium, Paulette Nardal and Les Nana Benz Terraces

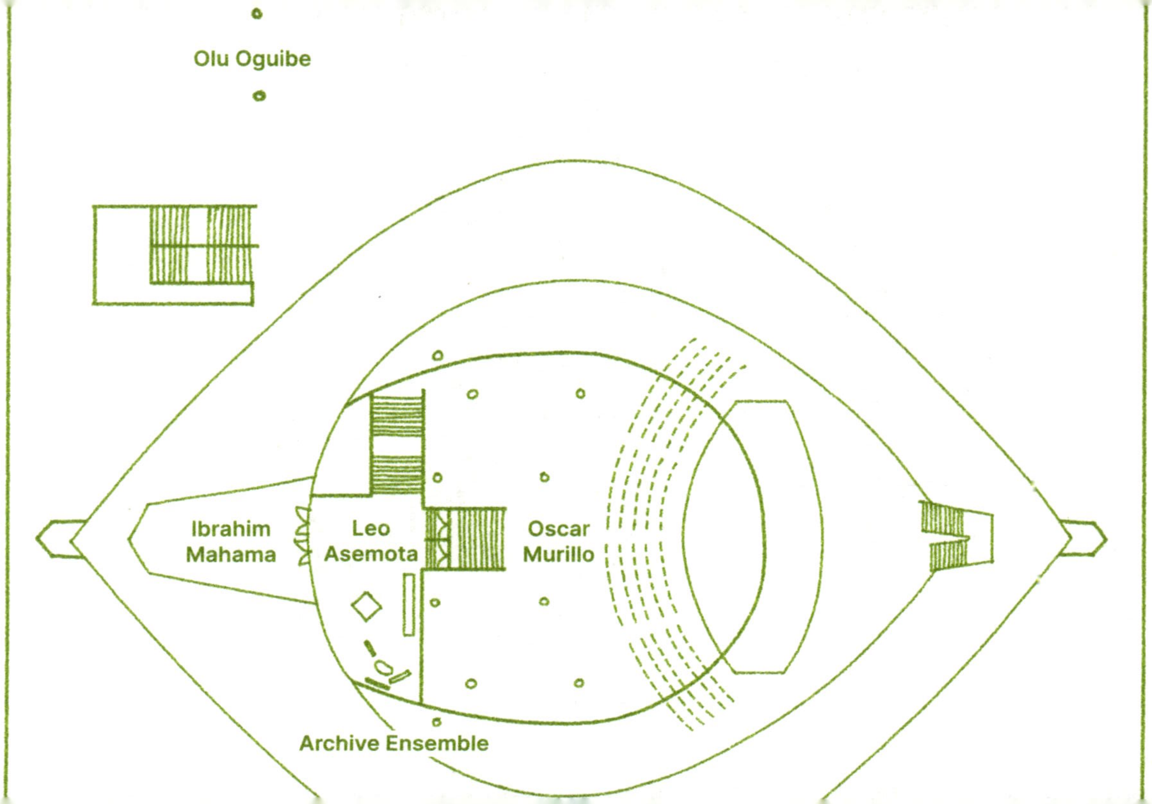
Olu Oguibe
Ibrahim Mahama
Leo Asemota
Oscar Murillo
Archive Ensemble

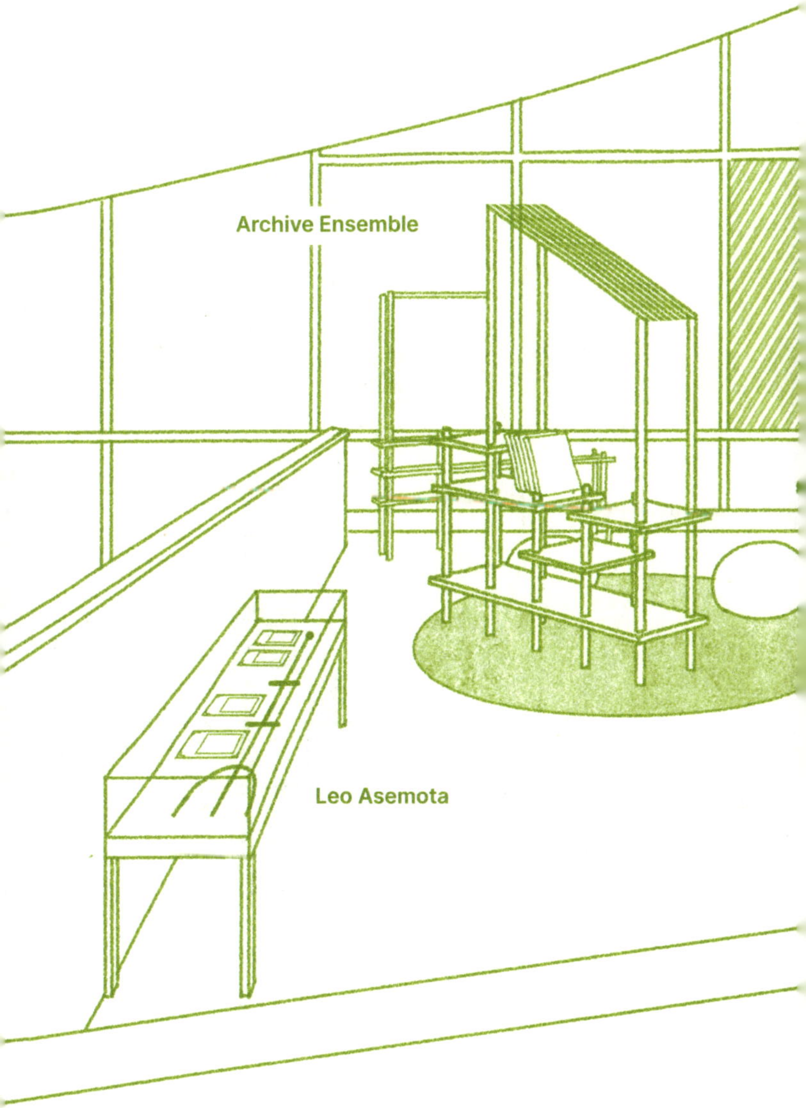

Archive Ensemble
Leo Asemota

Leo Asemota

Edo native, lives in London,
UK and Benin City, Nigeria

Leo Asemota

For *O Quilombismo*, Leo Asemota constructs a work drawn primarily from Yoruba knowledge values of *ìmò* (experience) and *òótó* (attestation) and Abdias Nascimento's *ABC of Quilombismo*. Its ideas fixate on three letters K, W, and Y, which are not used in Brazilian Portuguese words except in *estrangerismos*, words borrowed from other languages. In the *ABC of Quilombismo*, Nascimento assigns the letters K to Kimbundu and Y to Yoruba to proclaim the origins and bond of Afro-Brazilians with African religious and cultural identity; Asemota assigns W to work to encapsulate the sense of labour and economy in Nascimento's ideology. —LA

Commissioned by Haus der Kulturen der Welt (HKW), co-produced by Leo Asemota and HKW, 2023

(H)-KWY ìmò **live artwork by Leo Asemota on Sunday, 4 June, 18:00, see p. 271.**

Work in the exhibition:
(H)-KWY: òótó **(2023):** ***Flight Path I: Within / Beyond*****, graphite and acrylic on paper in gold blocked titled green Nigerian goatskin sketch holder with gold gilt corners, 14 × 22 cm;** ***Flight Path II: Star*** **(2023), graphite on paper in gold blocked titled green Nigerian goatskin sketch holder with gold gilt corners, 14 × 22 cm;** ***Flight Path III: NE / SW*** **(2023), graphite on paper in gold blocked titled green Nigerian goatskin sketch holder with gold gilt corners, 14 × 22 cm;** ***Flight Path IV: NW*** **(2023), graphite on paper in gold blocked titled green Nigerian goatskin sketch holder with gold gilt corners, 14 × 22 cm;** ***Flight Path V: Deep South*** **(2023), graphite on paper in gold blocked titled green Nigerian goatskin sketch holder with gold gilt corners, 14 × 22 cm;** ***Exu and Ogum (After Abdias do Nascimento)*** **(2023), wrought iron, 50 × 170 cm;** ***Primer*****, Orhue (kaolin) and gold leaf, dimensions vary. Other material: ten palm fronds, orhue (kaolin) on Brazilian timber, 30 × 45 cm; Four screens with HD color films and sound (with the unedited video recording of** ***ìmò*** **recurring at 18:00 daily at the exact time at which the live artwork was originally presented)**
Courtesy of the artist

Primer, Orhue (kaolin) and gold leaf
Photo: Courtesy of the artist / EoTLA

Archive Ensemble

Leila Bencharnia, Omar Gabriel Delnevo, Chiara Figone, Gabriella Rebello Kolandra, Giordana Pieri, Vanessa Vieira

Archive Ensemble reimagines libraries as communal displays for collective interaction and various cultural formats based on anti-colonial and feminist thinking and practice. In the *Haptic Library*, Archive Ensemble creates a library as a social display of texts to sense, touch, and listen to—a collection of *texturalities*. Using readings, textiles, and music as multi-sensorial mediums for archiving and disseminating narratives and knowledges, the *Haptic Library* redirects its focus beyond the printed book and the western dominant sense of sight towards the sense of touch, inviting us to relate to knowledge from a plurality of materialities and modes of thought—involving carpets, fabrics, sonicities, and printed media. Against the 'colonial library' that accumulates knowledge produced by the Eurocentric gaze, as defined by Congolese philosopher Valentin-Yves Mudimbe, the *Haptic Library* instead features plural perspectives and forms of story-telling across regions, generations, and epistemologies. As a space, the *Haptic Library* offers hospitality for one's own body in relation to a communal gathering. It includes various texturalities related to the research on the aesthetic and political genealogies of the *O Quilombismo* exhibition, such as publications from IPEAFRO (The Institute of Research and Afro-Brazilian Studies) founded by Abdias Nascimento in 1981 to practise the communitarian and affirmative philosophy of *quilombismo*. —PG

HKW wishes to sincerely thank SAVVY.DOC for their collaboration.

Work in the exhibition:
Haptic Library (2023), social display of texturalities (mixed materials) with readings, textiles, and sound, dimensions vary
Courtesy of Archive Ensemble

Oscar Murillo

1986, La Paila, Colombia, lives in various locations

Oscar Murillo

Disregarding semiotic hierarchies, Oscar Murillo articulates a wide range of media traditions (socially engaged and participatory projects included), cross-referencing different contexts and histories. For the exhibition, Murillo extends into sculptures the automatic-drawing-like practice he has developed over the years aboard planes. *Flight Drawings* is an installation of hung baked corn and concrete rock-like loafs, often present in his work, recurrently associated with toil and sustenance. In clusters held together by geometrical metal structures, they appear in conjunction with glass from the island of Murano in the Venetian lagoon, a reference to histories of tightly controlled markets and craftsmanship. The flocks of dense yet lightweight constellations of 'stones', suspended in the auditorium of the former congress hall that is now HKW, build on the symbolic associations of flight: mobility, geopolitics, borders, and identity. Addressing the governance of space, the installation stresses the tension between confinement and transgression, the organic and the man-made. Murillo anchors this work in his own family background: in the accompanying sound piece *My name is Belisario*, he broadcasts in a multitude of languages his father's testimony of migration from La Paila to the US, escaping an assassination attempt due to his union involvement, finally arriving to London. —A

Commissioned by Haus der Kulturen der Welt (HKW), co-produced by Oscar Murillo and HKW, 2023.

Industrial Park, a performance by Oscar Murillo, takes place on 9 July and 17 September. *For the Souls of the Rotten Mighty: Mar, Rio y Cordillera*, a band-in-residence project by Oscar Murillo runs from 30 July–12 August. For further information visit www.hkw.de.

flight #67 (2018), pen, pencil, graphite, carbon on Japanese paper, 28.5 × 39.5 cm. Photo: Tony Prikryl

Works in the exhibition:
Flight Drawings (2023), site-specific installation made of corn, cement, copper wire, steel and Murano glass; *My name is Belisario* (2015), sound installation in eighteen languages, eighteen sound recordings including Spanish, English, Igbo, Somali, and Farsi, approx. 15 minutes each
Courtesy of the artist

Ibrahim Mahama

Olu Oguibe

1987, Tamale, Ghana, lives there

Ibrahim Mahama

For the past decade, Ibrahim Mahama has been interested in objects in a state of decay, transforming them to explore themes of migration, globalization, and economic exchange in relation to the history of Ghana. His large-scale installations employ materials gathered from urban environments, junkyards, or abandoned buildings. These can include remnants of wood, metal, or jute sacks, but also historical textiles that transmit previously silenced memories and stories. In realizing *E PAIN ME* as well as *IN THE GARDEN*, the two sculptural tapestries he puts in conversation with HKW's historic architecture, Mahama employs stitching techniques inspired by traditional weaving practices widely found across West Africa. In creating these canvases of memory, he poetically engages in a healing process while unearthing and translating their embedded knowledges to a contemporary audience. From the junkyard owners who collect objects in decay to the weavers the artist invites as co-makers, collaboration is essential to the realization of the work. Mahama places a strong importance on passing down skills and memory through artistic creation, aiming to shift paradigms of education and knowledge circulation while also performing collective acts of rewriting history. MHP

Commissioned by Haus der Kulturen der Welt (HKW), co-produced by Ibrahim Mahama; Red Clay Studio, Tamale; and HKW, 2023.

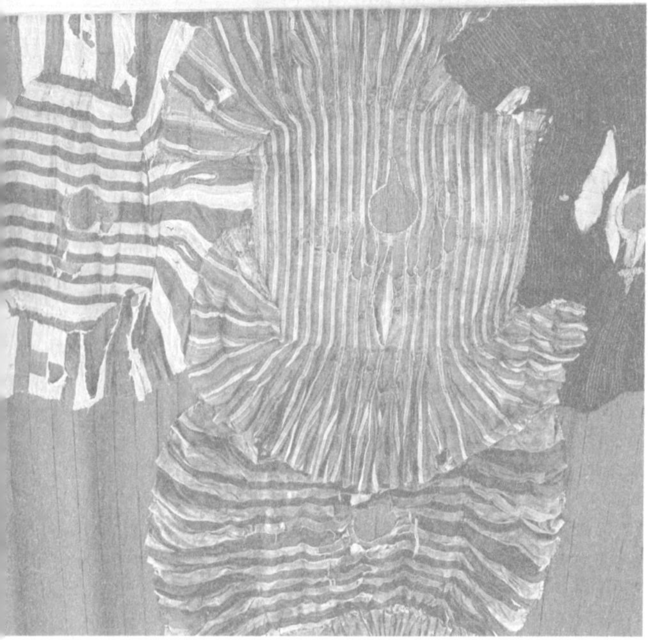

E PAIN ME. Photos: the artist

Works in the exhibition:
E PAIN ME (2023), installation of historical hand-woven fabrics, synthetic cotton, 20 × 30 m (Les Nana Benz Terrace); *IN THE GARDEN* (2023), installation of historical hand-woven fabrics, synthetic cotton, 19,6 × 4,5 × 19,1 × 9,1 m (Anna Seghers and Semra Ertan Gardens). Courtesy of the artist; Apalazzo Gallery, Brescia; White Cube Gallery, London, Hong Kong, New York, Paris, West Palm Beach; and Red Clay Studio, Tamale

Olu Oguibe

As a poet and visual artist, words, their meaning and what they perform, are fundamental to Olu Oguibe's work. For O *Quilombismo*, he was commissioned to create three flags to fly on HKW's terrace, visible from the nearby Government District. Carrying the colours black, red, gold, and green, Oguibe's flags are a poetic reference to the Pan-African flag, the First Nations flag, and the German flag. As Marcus Garvey pointed out: black represents the people, green stands for the land, red for the blood of African peoples spilled through enslavement and colonization, and yellow or gold for the wealth stolen. According to Oguibe, these colours are not only interesting because some feature on the German flag, but because these combinations come up when the ruling political parties have to form coalition governments: 'traffic light' coalition, 'Jamaica' coalition, 'Kenya' coalition. Embroidered on the flags are the letters DDR that stand for Decarbonize, Decolonize, Reparate (Repatriate or Rehabilitate). The latter highlights the necessity to reverse our carbon footprint, to thoroughly decolonize politically, materially, and mentally, and to repatriate what was stolen from colonized societies, repair what was destroyed, and rehabilitate the societies and cultures that have been transgressed upon. —BN

Commissioned by Haus der Kulturen der Welt (HKW), co-produced by Olu Oguibe and HKW, 2023.

Work in the exhibition:
DDR: Decarbonize, Decolonize, Rehabilitate
(2023), textile work, 3 flags, 4.5 × 7 m each
Courtesy of the artist

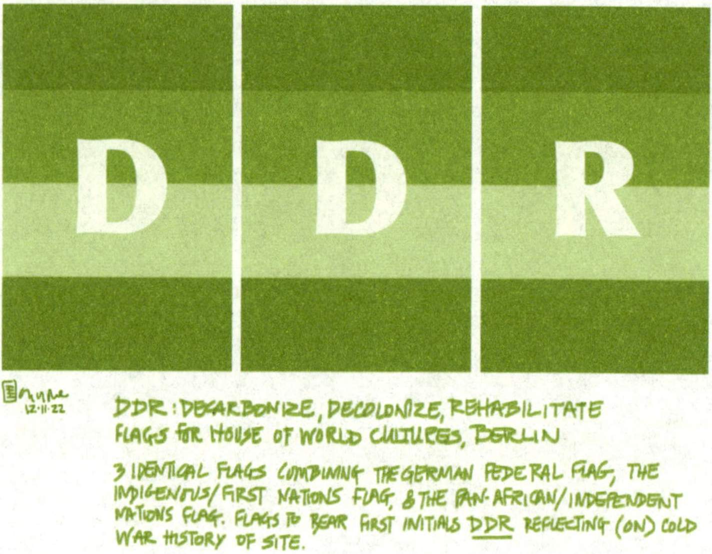

Study for *DDR: Decarbonize, Decolonize, Rehabilitate*, 2022

Lili Elbe Garden

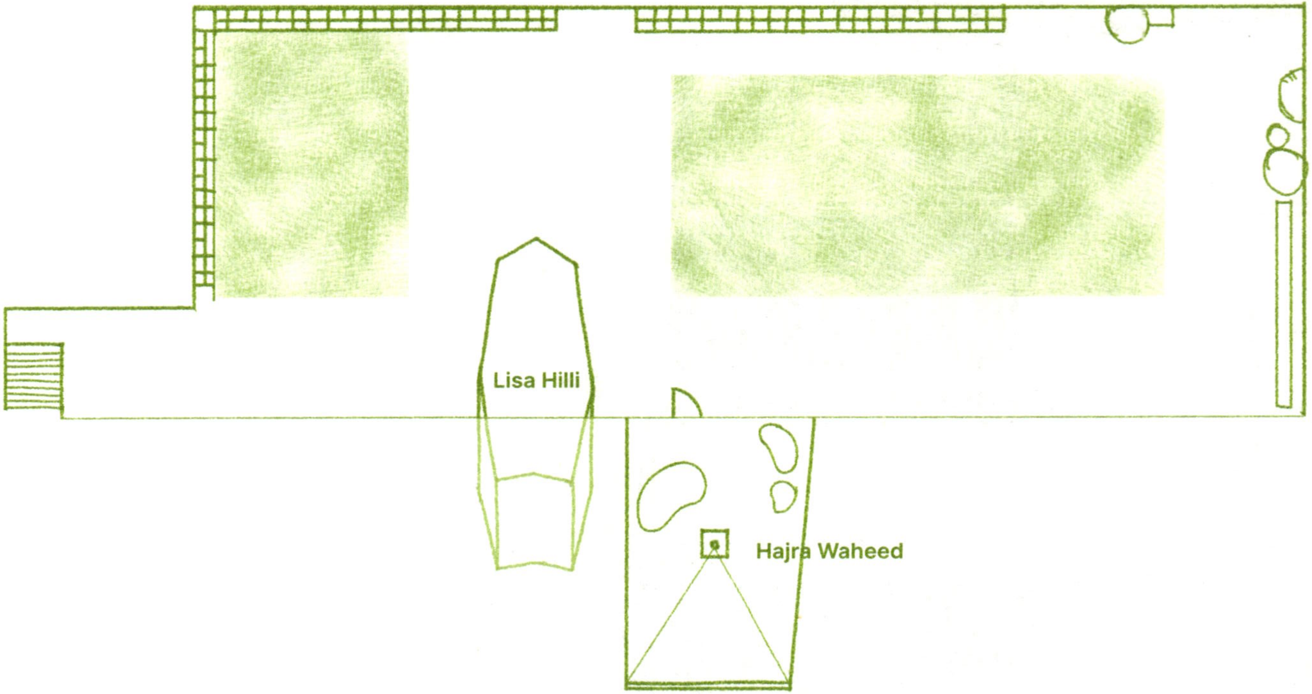
Lisa Hilli
Hajra Waheed

Hajra Waheed

Lisa Hilli

1979, Rabaul, Papua New Guinea, lives in Narrm [Melbourne], Australia

Lisa Hilli

Australian and Papua Niuginian (New Guinean) multidisciplinary artist, educator, and researcher Lisa Hilli highlights the (in)visibility of Black and Melanesian women, through photography, video, textiles, and installations with a historical sensitivity to different languages, tools, and formats. Drawing in part from her autobiography as a Tolai/Gunantuna woman, her story becomes interwoven with the agency of Papua Niuginian women, and their struggles. *Keep Your Bush Knife Sharp #BrukimBus* acknowledges the Melanesian women that bring about their own change through a series of intervened archival materials such as political history posters showing the vibrancy of resistances led by Papua Niuginian women during the 1960s and 70s, a time of radical activism in the Pacific Island nations and globally, including the Kafaina and Nilai Ra Varden movements. As part of Hilli's ongoing research and civic engagement, the posters are shown in print and via social media, situating them in a broader dynamic of circulating Oceanic knowledges. These reworked images become a visual narrative centred on the *meri blaus* (women's blouse), a dress appropriated from missionary influence, made and worn by everyday, grassroots women of Papua Niugini. Meri blaus making continues to be a viable skill and form of economic income for women across Melanesia, using textiles as an unexpected yet central form of knowledge. —AOW

Commissioned by Haus der Kulturen der Welt (HKW), co-produced by Lisa Hilli and HKW, 2023.

Work in the exhibition:
Keep Your Bush Knife Sharp #BrukimBus **(2023), series of intervened photographs, prints, dimensions vary**
Courtesy of the artist

Digital collage-sketch for *Keep Your Bush Knife Sharp #BrukimBus*

Hajra Waheed

This poetic video work begins with a compelling statement by the artist: 'The spiral is much more than just a form.' Universal and ubiquitous, centrifugal and centripetal, representing both growth and decay, spirals are one of the most widespread forms found in nature. The work grants us insight into the consciousness of the self and the expansion of this awareness outwards—a springboard for reflecting on individual upheaval and collective human experience. The film builds upon Hajra Waheed's existing practice of mapping patterns of colonial and state violence, acting as a meditation on *change* while reminding us of the importance of maintaining the long view, especially in relation to social transformation. —CS

Work in the exhibition:
The Spiral **(2019), video installation, 7' 10"**
Courtesy of the artist

Installation view, The Power Plant, Toronto, 2019. Photo: Toni Hafkensheid

Acts of Opening Again:

A Choreography of Conviviality

Nous nous connaissons en
foule, dans l'inconnu qui
ne terrifie pas. Nous crions
le cri de poésie. Nos barques
sont ouvertes, pour tous
nous les naviguons.

—Édouard Glissant,
Poétique de la Relation

Aligning with the onset of the new year in the Yoruba calendar, Haus der Kulturen der Welt (HKW) re-opens from 2 to 4 June 2023 with a series of blessings, concerts, lectures, performances, processions, readings, and rituals as well as the launch of the exhibition project *O Quilombismo: Of Resisting and Insisting. Of Flight as Fight. Of Other Democratic Egalitarian Political Philosophies*. Taking a cue from the history of the institution as a *Kongresshalle* (congress hall) inaugurated in 1957 before becoming HKW in 1989, we bring to the fore cultures of congressing—etymologically, cultures of walking together—implying practices of communality, hospitality, and the values of plurality.

Acts of Opening Again is thus a set of offerings and considerations of what needs to be surrendered and what needs to be upheld for us to thrive together in 'la casa grande' (the big house, the planet). It is a welcoming of those holding cultural and community wisdoms, as well as an unlocking of the gates for the spirits, the ancestors, our bodies and souls to come in and inhabit the space. It is granting room for laughter, dancing, flirting, eating, getting upset, or sad—room to move and be moved. A space of opening up to each other, to perfect imperfection, to the vulnerability and power of our presence. A house in which hope is practised together, as much as radical respect, humility, and love.

Activating the archives of our bodies and the centrality of the corporeal as a site of discourse and social transformation, HKW enlivens the performative practices programme by opening up spaces of expression and encounter for a plurality of bodies: physical bodies; contextual bodies; long uninvited bodies that are loud and have always reclaimed their rights to be present, that have waited to be heard for far too long; spiritual bodies; and the bodies of plants, trees, air, lands, and waters that constitute witnesses of all ages. Our spirits are constantly there. Invisible but visible, silent but speaking. They can engage us in conversations, excavating affects from the past to better express our present conditions, and create healed and healing futures.

Knowing, on the other hand, that the body is the very first space of sovereignty, on its opening weekend HKW invites all to experience visual, sonic, sensorial, and choreographed narrations of being together and to draw inspiration from the philosophy and practising of the plural performativities of quilombismo.

Marie Helene Pereira and
Carlos Maria Romero aka Atabey

Programme

Exhibition Opening Times
Fri 2 June from 17:00–23:00
and Sat 3 & Sun 4 June
from 12:00–23:00

Childcare (free of charge)
Available 2 June from 17:00–20:00
and 3 & 4 June from 12:00–20:00

Please register via education@hkw.de
and indicate the number of children
and their age(s).

Throughout the Opening

RELEASE: a living ritual for letting go (2023)
vanessa german

Participatory Performance / Score, 'Cards of release' available at the counter, Sylvia Wynter Foyer

Take a card, an invitation from the artist to partake in an intentional stroll upon the land where HKW is located.

> With every step, breath, blink of an eye and beat of a heart upon this land ... we bring release to the stories held in captivity, submerged, silenced or otherwise unvoiced[.] ... In this way, we make an offering ... a cleared path for which to joy in the creation of spaces[.] We become these offerings with ease and grace.

vanessa german (see p. 62) gifts visitors, upon a small card, language for a communal, connected release of any energetic blockages, voices, pains, or songs from the built and natural spaces within and around HKW as a home of heart and creativity. These 'cards of release' are made out of paper pulped with flower seeds. The 'release' manifests not only through the actions of each individual but is also offered to the earth as the seeds transform into new blooms. —A

Commissioned by Haus der Kulturen der Welt (HKW), co-produced by vanessa german and HKW, 2023.

For vanessa german's participatory walk, *Hand in Hand: a love poem for togetherness*, see p. 263.

Fri 2 June, 17:00–20:00
Sat 3 & Sun 4 June 12:00–20:00

El Medán (2012–ongoing)
Bernardo Oyarzún

Participatory Performance and Installation

The 'medán' is an ancestral Mapuche community celebration of reciprocity that is still practised today in the southern Chilean island of Chiloé. In situations of need or in support of starting a new home, the celebration calls in the surrounding community to help provide for a new venture. Medán simply translates to 'they give me' in Spanish—people contribute with their labour, farm animals, seeds, or household artefacts to ignite the well-being of a dwelling, while the host offers a convivial experience. For the re-opening of HKW, artist Bernardo Oyarzún proposes an artistic *Medán,* inviting Berlin communities to participate in the making of HKW as a home, bringing symbolic offerings and co-creating a performative installation during the three-day inaugural festival. The public is encouraged to join in on this installation with creative gestures in the form of a token of kindness, poem, song, or artistic gift. —PG/A

See the full call at www.hkw.de.

Kilombo: Piwuchen, sculpture by Bernardo Oyarzùn, see p. 104.

Friday 2 June

16:00
Welcome in front of Haus der Kulturen der Welt (HKW)
by **Prof Dr Bonaventure Soh Bejeng Ndikung**

16:30
Invoking Papa Legba (2023)
Houngan Jean-Daniel Lafontant with **Claude Saturne**

Ceremonial Opening

HKW's reopening festival begins by invoking Papa Legba, the gate opener, guardian of crossroads, and intermediary between a spiritual dimension and the telluric worlds, convened by the *Sèvitè Houngan* [Vodou priest], Jean-Daniel Lafontant. Lafontant is the co-founder and guardian of the sacred temple Na-Ri-VéH 777 located in Port-au-Prince, Haiti. For more than two decades Lafontant has produced and helped shape a plentitude of documentary films, art exhibitions, articles, conferences, projects, and events on Haitian art and culture, striving to understand Vodou in its spiritual, philosophical, and cultural manifestations.

Vodou is a worldview fusing diverse African traditions, including West African Vodun religion, that is still carried out today by the descendants of the Dahomean, Kongo, and Yoruba people. The culture, traditions, and spiritual practices of the Indigenous Taíno, enslaved in their territory, are also an integral part of Vodou. Later, in colonial Saint-Domingue, as Haiti was called then, the Vodou-vi even took elements from Christianity and other colonial institutions and used them in their practices. To date, some Catholic imagery is a proxy for the ancestral *Lwa* or Vodou spirits. Vodou is a philosophy, science, and medicine, as well as a healing, religious, and judicial-political system that encompasses strong spiritual beliefs rooted in nature and ancestry. —A

Commissioned by Haus der Kulturen der Welt (HKW), co-produced by Houngan Jean-Daniel Lafontant, Claude Saturne, and HKW, 2023.

When We Gather (2022)
María Magdalena Campos-Pons, Baba Murah & Ensemble, Forum Brasil and **Ilê Obá Sileké, Candomblé House in Berlin,** and **Rasiel Almanza Cairo**

Performance

In the tradition of renewal rituals, the performance *When We Gather* invokes ancestral beings and knowledge to bring benevolence and vitality into the space of HKW. Cuban artist María Magdalena Campos-Pons asks what needs to be given up in order to accommodate a culture rooted in peace, hope, and togetherness. With Baba Murah, practitioners of the local Candomblé House, the Afro-Brazilian cultural forum, a Cuban Santería priest, and Bata drummer Rasiel Almanza Cairo, they summon, in a procession accompanied by chants and other invocations, *orishas* (divine forces of nature for the Yoruba) and other good energies to inhabit the space in support of this process. —A

Prayer Flags, installation by María Magdalena Campos-Pons, see p. 38.

18:00
Opening Speeches
(in German and English with simultaneous translation)

Claudia Roth, Minister of State for Culture and the Media
Prof Dr Bonaventure Soh Bejeng Ndikung, Director and Chief Curator, HKW
Victoria Tauli-Corpuz, founder and Executive Director of Tebtebba Foundation (Indigenous Peoples' International Centre for Policy Research and Education), 2014–20 UN Special Rapporteur on Indigenous Peoples' Rights

19:00
NOT waiting... (2023)
nora chipaumire and **Germaine Acogny**

Performance

From what started as a residency in Dakar in 2022 now comes to Berlin as a newly commissioned performance. Choreographers nora chipaumire and Germaine Acogny put forth an act of refusal, of intergenerational conversation and transmission, and of sorority and solidarity—a political statement and gesture that promotes ongoing practices found in Senegal and Zimbabwe. Drawing inspiration from the history of the Lébou community and the central place that women have in the traditional Ndeup healing ceremony, chipaumire and Acogny are accompanied and guided by a sonic ensemble played by five women from Toubab Dialaw, a coastal village of fishermen in Senegal, recalling the chants that connect them to the water spirits who bring healing blessings to the community. —MHP

Commissioned by Haus der Kulturen der Welt (HKW), co-produced by nora chipaumire, HKW, and RAW Material Company, supported by African Makers and Martine de Limburg, 2023.

19:30
Dine on a Mat—A Taste from the Fulani Kitchen
Chef Fatmata Binta

Describing herself as a nomadic chef, Fatmata Binta was born and raised in Freetown, Sierra Leone to a family of Guinean descent. She has been investigating the kitchen of the Fula people, one of the greatest nomadic groups of the African continent. While serving her own culinary creations paired with grains, spices, and ingredients from West Africa, she discusses Fulani history and culture. As a child, Chef Binta was fascinated by the chains of solidarity formed by her community during moments of limited food resources. The joy of her people coming together inspired Chef Binta to learn to make new dishes with local ingredients like Fonio grains. Looking to the future, she has gained enough experience and resources that she has been able to start a foundation, Empowering Fulani Women. —MHP

Limited number of participants; tickets available at www.hkw.de.

20:30
Awilo Longomba

Concert

The opening weekend's musical journey starts with the Congolese rumba, whose roots are connected to West and Central African sonic imaginaries and are affiliated with son cubano and jazz. This musical genre, played by many bands in the Democratic Republic of Congo, is very important for the history and development of music worldwide, and has been recognized as a World Intangible Cultural Heritage due to its pan-African values and contribution to African memory. Also stemming from Congolese rumba, soukous is a high energy, faster tempo, and highly danceable genre, which conserves elements of rock, gospel, and soul in the history of its development. Techno-soukous, a variant of soukous, is showcased by legendary musician Awilo Longomba and his band. —EM

22:00
SNO

DJ Set

Selina Nongaliphe Oliphant aka DJ SNO grew up in the Bophelong township in the Vaal, South Africa and is based in Manchester. Her music is a very personal sonic depiction of music from the African continent—joyful, eclectic, and unique.

00:00
Edna Martinez

DJ Set

Edna Martinez's sets are characterized by rhythms that narrate the musical journey between the territories known as Africa, the Caribbean, and the Levant, and in particular, in the sounds found in *cultura picotera* (picó sound system culture) from the Colombian Caribbean where she grew up.

Saturday 3 June

12:00
Artistic Practices in Conversation:
A Curatorial Walk Through the Exhibition
Cosmin Costinaş, Paz Guevara, Marie Helene Pereira, Carlos Maria Romero aka Atabey, Prof Dr Bonaventure Soh Bejeng Ndikung, and present **artists**

Exhibition Walk
(in English)

13:00–15:00 & 18:00–20:00
Hand in Hand: a love poem for togetherness (2023)
vanessa german

Participatory Walk, 1–5 people at a time, 11',
registration at counter, Sylvia Wynter Foyer

With a definitive place of arrival in mind, vanessa german (see p. 62) offers a guided walk, carried by the creative tide of intuition, over the land and through public spaces that comprise HKW—a living home to imagine and forge together. It is an offering of simple, but intimate connection: let us walk hand in hand and see what happens. Are we the same at the beginning of the walk as we are upon its conclusion? How do we mark one another in our time and proximity? How do tenderness and intimate connection bond us to the land? How might we come to know ourselves *at home* here? In this brief journey, one may find co-creation happens along the way as well as engagement with the surroundings, however that may manifest. —A

Commissioned by Haus der Kulturen der Welt (HKW), co-produced by vanessa german and HKW, 2023.

For vanessa german's participatory performance/score *RELEASE: a living ritual for letting go*, see p. 257.

13:00
Subversive Bodies in Conversation:
Bodies as Joyfields, Bodies as Battlefields
O'Neil Lawrence, Bruno Zhu, and **Grada Kilomba**

Conversation

Drawing on their practice, background, and research, the speakers engage in a conversation on bodies that resist representation and metaphor, while healing from histories and patterns of abuse and invisibility. O'Neil Lawrence, artist, writer, researcher, and Chief Curator of the National Gallery of Jamaica brings to the table his research work on genealogies of representing Black masculinized queer bodies, Bruno Zhu (see. p. 136) contributes perspectives on his own artistic work engaging with queerness, racism, migration, and the multiple skins one negotiates on a daily basis, while Grada Kilomba (see p. 118), artist and co-curator of this year's Biennial of São Paulo, speaks of her practice of storytelling centred around concepts of memory, trauma, gender, and post-colonialism, disrupting the collective discourse through an urgent decolonial language and imagery.

14:00
Restitution in Conversation: Feminist Perspectives on Restitution Beyond Ownership
Tuli Mekondjo, Hermosa Intervención, and **Lisa Hilli**

Conversation

Tuli Mekondjo, Hermosa Intervención, and Lisa Hilli deliberate on feminist perspectives on restitution that reimagine it outside of limiting frames of institutional ownership, and the western obsession of preservation. Instead, they consider questions of loss and restoration, memory and recreation, and embodiment and socialization. Working with and against colonial archives, Tuli Mekondjo (see. p. 86) presents her ongoing artistic work and social commitment to bringing back to life fertility dolls that were no longer created and shared during German colonization in Namibia. The Afro-Uruguayan female collective Hermosa Intervención (see. p. 134) discusses the pervasive racist narratives present within their community and the need to reconstruct and perform neglected Afro-Latina experiences and histories to resist and transform neo-colonial hegemony. Lisa Hilli (see. p. 248) digs into the histories of resistance of female-led movements in Melanesia, reflecting upon them as precursors of contemporary struggles and foregrounding the (in)visibility of Black and Melanesian women.

15:00
The Dawn Incantations III (2023)
Tanka Fonta with **Eden Meier** and **Saliou Cissokho**

Sound Performance

In the central rotunda of HKW, artist Tanka Fonta painted a circular score, an emerging mural work and picto-sonic composition of nine thematic movements orchestrated in evocative languages as visual, sonic, and poetic imprints. These visual scores are activated through sounds and movements led by dancer and choreographer Eden Meier and kora player Saliou Cissokho. Knowing that the associations of music to colour are mediated by emotion, Fonta and his orchestra invite the audience to a meditative journey punctuated by the sonicity of the kora strings, Meier's moving body, as well as the motion embedded in his visual circular score. —MHP

Commissioned by Haus der Kulturen der Welt (HKW), co-produced by Tanka Fonta and HKW, 2023.

> *The Cosmogenic Interconnectedness 'How Did We Talk Before The Roman Alphabet?' The Picto-Sonic Dialogues I*, mural by Tanka Fonta, see p. 56.

15:00–17:00
Children's discoteque at raumlaborberlin Pavilion

16:00
Between Revolution and Repair: Rereading Walter Rodney's How Europe Underdeveloped Africa
David Scott

Keynote Lecture

In the context of the current political demands to reflect upon centuries of colonization, how should one reread and re-engage with Walter Rodney's 1972 text *How Europe Underdeveloped Africa*? Are there questions about history and politics that need to be rethought in order to produce a critical relationship to such a text? Rodney's book emerged in the context of the African (and Caribbean) socialist revolution. In a sense, not only the historical but also the conceptual conditions of that project have collapsed. Revolution is no longer a self-evident telos, politically or even organizationally. Can we rethink the ideas about social change embedded in *How Europe Underdeveloped Africa* so as to connect them to contemporary conceptions of a radical reparatory politics? —DS

David Scott is Professor of Anthropology at Columbia University, New York, US.

Save the Date:
Further Events with David Scott

Fri., 9 June
18:00–22:00
The Sonic Vernacular: Blackness, Sound, and Fugitivity

Screenings, Performance Lecture with **David Scott**

Framed by two films, visitors can listen to selections of 1960s and 70s Jamaican music from ska to reggae, while David Scott talks about the music and its contexts.

In collaboration with the RTG Minor Cosmopolitanisms, University of Potsdam, where Scott is a Mercator Fellow for the summer.

Negus – Lee 'Scratch' Perry
Invernomuto, Italy 2013, 11', Jamaican English

Embodied through Lee 'Scratch' Perry—godfather of dub music and foundational to the sound and culture of reggae—the film explores the convergence of history, myth, and magic through the ambivalent and manifold legacies of Ethiopia's last emperor Haile Selassie I.

A David Scott Playlist
Performance Lecture

Taking on different forms of violence across the globe, colonialism has shaped not only infrastructure, resource distribution, and politics, but also the sonic environments that engage and connect people and movements. During the age of formal decolonization, music and musicians from colonized spaces were first and foremost activists and used their art to express anti-colonial visions for the future. Their music was, and must be considered as, part of the anti-colonial struggle. Together with Jamaican anthropologist David Scott, visitors take a journey through the ska and reggae soundscapes of 1960s and 70s Jamaica to explore how they shaped and accompanied movements of liberation.

PICO: Un Parlante de África en América
Invernomuto, Jim Christopher Nedd, Italy/USA 2017, 60', Spanish with English subtitles

This documentary film explores the extravagant cultural richness of the *picó* tradition: wooden structures covered in striking painted artworks, which house the powerful sound systems that animate the streets, bars, and restaurants in the Afro-Colombian cities of Barranquilla and Cartagena.

Fri., 7 July
16:00–20:00
on movement(s) and collective(s)—Black Radicals in/and Berlin

Keynote Conversation

Radical movements strive for transformative solidarity amid difference and across locations while situating and grounding their collective actions within local strengths, needs, and struggles. In this conversation, David Scott and antiracist groups in Berlin discuss contemporary triumphs and challenges of Black radical movements across various locations, how international struggles connect to the local, and how concepts translate into practice.

A partnership between HKW, the RTG Minor Cosmopolitanisms at the University of Potsdam, and the Amo Collective at the Institute for European Ethnology, Humboldt-Universität zu Berlin.

17:00
O Quilombismo Reader

Book Launch
(in English)

The publication engages with the founding figures and initial conceptual articulations of *quilombismo*, but also explores how it has found resonance in disparate practices globally. Contributors to the volume discuss its trajectories and perspectives. For more information about the reader see p. 278.

18:00
Neptune Frost
Saul Williams and **Anisia Uzeyman**, 2021, Rwanda/US, 110', Kinyarwanda, Kirundi, Swahili, French, English with English subtitles

Screening

In Burundi, a group of escaped coltan miners form an anti-colonial hacker collective with one declared aim in mind: to overthrow the exploitative regime. An intersex runaway and a miner find their way to each other by means of cosmic powers—a contact that results in a disruption to the more-than-human cycle. In lyrical hymns and songs, which alternate between Kinyarwanda, Kirundi, Swahili, English, and French, the film questions sexual and cultural identity, western hegemony, reality, and the past and present. *Neptune Frost* is an Afrofuturist masterpiece, a musical plea for a future in which technology is used for liberatory political and social purposes.

20:30

Oumou Sangaré

Concert

With Malian star Oumou Sangaré, West African music comes into focus—a kaleidoscope of many genres using percussion, polyrhythms, traditional instruments, and modern sounds with resonance in different parts of the Americas in the form of boogie, makossa, funk, samba, zouk, and more. The singer's album *Moussolou* sold more than 250,000 copies in its first 1991 edition alone, and today some of her songs are considered hymns far beyond the African continent. Sangaré, who has collaborated with global pop stars like Beyoncé and Aya Nakamura, presents a unique show which blends Wassoulou tradition with modern instrumentation from a feminist and socially-engaged perspective. —EM

22:00

Katerinha & Njeri

DJ Set

A Berlin-based DJ duo consisting of Macedonian musician/creative producer Katerinha and Kenyan newcomer Njeri, their sound is a soulful crossover of RnB, jazz, afro house, garage, breaks, and eclectic club sounds.

00:00

MSJY

DJ Set

MSJY, producer and DJ with several cultural influences, is willing to provocatively unwind the norms and push the narrative. A deliberately shapeshifting persona, she explores iridescent soundscapes through her sets that dig into bass and breaks, adding dashes of trip-hop and IDM along the way.

Sunday 4 June

12:00

Muralism in Conversation: A Walk Through the Murals
Tanka Fonta, Nontsikelelo Mutiti, Alberto Pitta, Paz Guevara,
and **Cosmin Costinaş**

Exhibition Walk
(in English)

Activating the social dimension of murals, the stories they can tell, and their multi-sensorial resonance, artists Tanka Fonta, Nontsikelelo Mutiti, and Alberto Pitta offer an invitation to walk through their murals in the exhibition together with curators Cosmin Costinaş and Paz Guevara. Tanka Fonta (see p. 56) opens up a conversational space, engaging the public to inhabit the mural as an 'artistic storytelling in visual and sonic form', discussing the non-western philosophical knowledges it disseminates. By intervening in the exhibition space with a mural that spreads depictions of braiding techniques across the floor, Nontsikelelo Mutiti (see p. 76) reinvigorates their political liberatory geometries and invites visitors to cross the exhibition space while collectively decoding histories of emancipation. From his silk-screen studio in Salvador de Bahia, Alberto Pitta (see p. 44) has transformed the facade of the HKW with a two-section mural featuring Yoruba deity Ogum and the communal housing of contemporary quilombos. Pitta hosts a visual storytelling session to delve into the spiritual, political, and visual dimensions of his work.

13:30

Quilombo Continuum
Juliana M. Streva, Brazil/Germany, 2023, 23', Brazilian Portuguese with English subtitles (European Premiere)

Screening followed by a conversation with **Juliana M. Streva, Zica Pires,** and **Carol Barreto**
(in English)

The experimental documentary *Quilombo, Continuum* interrupts and challenges the myths of social cohesion and racial democracy in Brazil. Combining archival material with statements from the Black Radical Tradition spoken by Beatriz Nascimento, Lélia Gonzalez, and Abdias Nascimento, as well as by the contemporary activists and politicians such as Erica Malunguinho, Debora Dias, Julio Cesar, and others, the film invites viewers to take a closer look at the practice of *quilombo*. The multitude of voices, practices, and memories the documentary encompasses offer a guide through the history of quilombos and their reactivation today.

The screening is followed by a conversation with the film-maker Juliana M. Streva and the artists Zica Pires (p. 192) and Carol Barreto (p. 214), moderated by Paz Guevara and Carlos Maria Romero aka Atabey. The participants comment on the film from their experience of contemporary struggles and knowledge of quilombos, considering their history and importance in asserting the rights of Afro-Brazilian people and the affirmation of culture in equal terms. —CS

15:00
Alejandra Saavedra Hernández

A walk through the exhibition (in German)

15:00
Bread Scores (2022)
Masimba Hwati and friends **Laura Anh Thu Dang, Luka Mukhavele, Lefteris Krysalis**

Performance

Zimbabwean artist Masimba Hwati convenes a bread-breaking ceremony to invoke the history of the *Chimurenga* (revolutionary uprising) and the Shona and Ndebele insurrections in former Rhodesia, now Zimbabwe. *Bread Scores* is a performative creation inspired by the smuggling of bread to political prisoners—fellow activists, relatives, and loved ones would send hidden newspaper clippings, information about the ongoing struggle, words of solidarity and support, and love letters to ease the solitude of those behind bars. Hwati hides musical scores inspired by traditional Chimurenga chants of resistance in loaves of bread and invites the musicians to create sonic interpretations thereof. —MHP

The performance is broadcast live on Cashmere Radio, Radio Submarine, and bauhaus.fm.

Dzikamunhenga 3 and *Dzikamunhenga 4*, sculptures by Masimba Hwati, see p. 116.

16:00–18:00
Children's discoteque at raumlaborberlin Pavilion

16:00
Archiving Marginalized Knowledge: Intersectional Black European Studies
Fatima El-Tayeb

Keynote (English with simultaneous translation into German

Fatima El-Tayeb is Professor of Ethnicity, Race & Migration and Women's, Gender, and Sexuality Studies at Yale University, New Haven, US. Her research interests include Black Europe, comparative diaspora studies, queer of colour critique, critical Muslim studies, decolonial theory, transnational feminisms, visual culture studies, race and technology, and critical European studies. She is the author of three books and numerous articles on the interactions of race, gender, sexuality, religion, and nation. Her current research projects explore the intersecting legacies of colonialism, fascism, and socialism in Europe and the potential of (queer) people of colour alliances in decolonizing the continent.

El-Tayeb's talk outlines the foundational critique of intersectional Black European studies, a discipline at the centre of the decolonization debate, taking HKW's 2004 *Black Atlantic* project as a point of departure for considering the relationship critical race studies has to the German context. Focusing on the continued seeming impossibility of Black Europeans, El-Tayeb talks about epistemic alignments, objectivity, and the necessity of archiving marginalized knowledge.

17:00
The Butterfly Effect
Simon Njami

Keynote Lecture (in English with simultaneous translation into German)

Simon Njami is a Paris-based independent curator, lecturer, art critic, and novelist. He was the co-founder and editor-in-chief of *Revue Noire*, a journal of contemporary African and extra-occidental art, and served as artistic director of the Bamako Encounters – African Biennale of Photography from 2001–7 and Dak'Art 2016/2018. His books include biographies of James Baldwin and Leopold Sédar Senghor, as well as four novels.

Njami's talk departs from John Foster Dulles, US Secretary of State between 1953 and 1959, and namesake of the street where HKW's building, which originally opened as the *Kongresshalle* (congress hall) in 1957, is located. Moving on to 1989, when the institution of HKW was conceived, he touches upon seemingly marginal phenomena that impact world history: the so-called butterfly effect. Picking up the core of the institution's name, 'World Cultures', he addresses notions of Otherness, the response to such stances by Africa and its cultural institutions, and finally deals with 'end of history' ideologies and the current debate on the restitution of cultural property stolen from the African continent under colonialism.

18:00
(H)-KWY ìmò (2023)
Leo Asemota

Live Artwork

(H)-KWY ìmò is a site-specific live artwork that sets in motion Leo Asemota's installation *òótó* (see p. 228). Emerging from the directions north, east, south, and west, four characters navigate their respective cardinal positions within HKW to a meeting point where they carry out an array of activities including Brazilian capoeira movements among other gestures. The ensuing installation *òótó* can be seen daily in its totality at 18:00, reoccurring at the exact time in which ìmò was originally presented, its ideas evolving over the course of the exhibition. —LA

Commissioned by Haus der Kulturen der Welt (HKW), co-produced by Leo Asemota and HKW, 2023.

(H)-KWY òótó by Leo Asemota, see p. 228.

19:00
Dine on a Mat—A Taste from the Fulani Kitchen
Chef Fatmata Binta

See programme for Friday, 19:30
Limited number of participants; tickets available at www.hkw.de.

20:30
Estrellas del Caribe

Concert

The final concert of the opening weekend explores the continuity of the Caribbean and the Americas, where strong legacies of Congolese music, but also Nigerian highlife and other rhythms of Africa remain present in the music of the *palenques* and *quilombos*. Outlining a solid connection to the Afro-Colombian legacy, the concert showcases Estrellas del Caribe, a group hailing from San Basilio de Palenque, the first free town in the Americas, performing in Berlin for the very first time. Their sound derives from the oral tradition of the first enslaved peoples that were brought to the country and connects to the 1970s, when the group was founded, with beats popularized through sound systems known as *picós*. —EM

Supported by the Embassy of the Republic of Colombia

22:00
mokeyanju

DJ Set

A passionate dancer, writer, and vinyl selector from Nigeria and based in Berlin, Jumoke Adeyanju aka mokeyanju is heavily influenced by Detroit's hip-hop and house music legacy, as well as fuji, highlife, ndombolo, and percussive music genres, and has a broad interest in East African and Caribbean culture.

Related Programme

After the re-opening festival, the project *O Quilombismo: Of Resisting and Insisting. Of Flight as Fight. Of Other Democratic Egalitarian Political Philosophies* continues with a rich programme of activities and articulations. In taking seriously the premise that there is much to be learned from the *quilombos* and quilombo-like spaces, the project insists that spaces of freedom—and freedom itself—must be continuously cultivated, brought into being, and conceived anew. The exhibition and the related performances, film screenings, concerts, storytelling assemblies, cooking sessions, lectures, and research and educational programmes are practices that enliven the heritage of solidarity and struggle of *quilombismo* as living culture.

For further details on the programme activities visit www.hkw.de.

For the Love of Liberty?
(En)Countering Franklin

Installation, 2023–2027

Opened in 1957 as a gift by the United States to West Berlin, HKW's building is an architectural icon of post-war western modernity. As a political symbol in the context of the Cold War, its ideologization is manifest in the architectural design as well as in a quote by US Founding Father Benjamin Franklin, who was an owner of enslaved people, and a beneficiary of the trading of them. Engraved on the walls of the Sylvia Wynter Foyer, it invokes the 'love of liberty' and the 'rights of man' to assert 'that a philosopher may set his foot anywhere on [the earth's] surface and say "this is my country"'. In the context of US imperialism, habitually legitimized by such claims, Franklin's latent endorsement of an entitled approach to the world's geographies has had far reaching implications. HKW seeks to delimit the violent and singular imperial vision inherent in the quote and actively question the paradigmatic implications of the semi-casual reference to the colonial playbook in the name of universalist values. Eight eminent figures across disciplines and geographies contributed their responses which are presented alongside Franklin's quote in the HKW foyer as part of a semi-permanent installation designed by Studio Yukiko.

Contributions by Hinemoana Baker, Omri Boehm, Erna Brodber, Ken Bugul, Ntone Edjabe, Pumla Dineo Gqola, Saša Stanišić, Françoise Vergès

Shaped to the Measure of the People's Songs
Annual Series of Pavilions, 2023–2027
in 2023 by **raumlaborberlin**

HKW presents a new series of annual temporary pavilions as artistic interventions in public space, offering a new space of encounter and experimentation at the interface between its historic building, the biotope of the Tiergarten, and the surrounding context of Berlin's urban and political fabric. Today's continuing crises around the climate, housing shortages, and exclusionary urban infrastructures re-emphasize the need for a concrete examination of spatial issues when envisioning collective ways of living. As a public, accessible, and open space, the pavilion is an artistic intervention and site of engagement beyond HKW's main building, enabling visitors and passersby to gather informally around and beyond its programme activities. The inaugural pavilion is designed and developed by the Berlin-based architecture collective raumlaborberlin. The basis of their design is Buckminster Fuller's *Dymaxion Map*—an experimental imagining he first developed in 1943, which projects the global map onto a polyhedral surface and triangulates its geography into an expanded and interconnected matrix. This visual exercise pushes against a reading of the globe as a cluster of separated and distinct entities and insists on the inseparability of our global geographies that demand communication, care, and solutions on a collaborative planetary scale.

Cultural Education Programmes

The programme accompanying the *O Quilombismo* exhibition invites the public into a dialogue. Barrier-free, inclusive formats, and workshops for families, as well as bookable group tours for different age groups are offered. For further dates and details visit www.hkw.de.

Each Saturday & Sunday
A Walk through the Exhibition With…

Working with light and sound, concepts, or printed materials, various members of the HKW team share their specific knowledge during walks through the exhibition and open up new perspectives on the works. With, among others: Prof Dr Bonaventure Soh Bejeng Ndikung, Director and Chief Curator / Henriette Gallus, Deputy Director / Cosmin Costinaş, Felix Fuchs, Paz Guevara, Lisa Xenia Ness, and Shohreh Shakoory from Exhibition Practices / Muhammad Ali Sözen from Exhibition Building and Construction / Julia Büki, Marie Helene Pereira, and Carlos Maria Romero aka Atabey from Performative Practices / Emilienne Fernande Bodo and Lama El Khatib from Architectural and Spatial Practices / Rosa Cordillera Castillo and Sara Morais dos Santos Bruss from Scientific, Digital, and Media Practices / Dzekashu MacViban and Alexandra Ortiz Wallner from Literature and Oralture Practices / Eric Otieno Sumba, Fiona Shipwright, and Jill Winder from Publication Practices / Çiğdem C. Kolain, Marine Lucina, Daniel Neugebauer, and Eva Stein from Cultural Education / Jan Trautmann from Communications

Each Monday, 15:00–18:00
Quilombismo Dialogues

What role does exhibition architecture play? Is it important where an exhibit comes from? What does the year of origin say about an artistic work?

Every Monday, alternately in English, German, Turkish, Spanish, Arabic, and Farsi, the *Quilombismo Dialogues* offer exhibition visitors the opportunity to exchange ideas with HKW mediators. The themes and narratives of the exhibition are questioned and deepened in a joint conversation based on the different interests, questions, and knowledge of those attending.

School of Quilombismo
3–4 June, 28–30 July, 26–31 August 2023

The *School of Quilombismo* aims to pay homage to friendships, histories, and networks that inhabit the energy, spirit, knowledge, and politics of marronage, anti-colonial troublemakers, and the *quilombo* to carry on the belief that radical forms of pedagogies can support how people navigate their everyday lives as well as the futures to come. In the spirit of the quilombo educators, nomadic cosmologists, fugitive scientists, and street philosophers, the school takes shape through performances, discussions, workshops, a night school, listening sessions, dance parties, and walks. Each communal gathering is itinerant and sometimes unsettling, informing zpearing (and disappearing) in several non-institutional and public spaces throughout Berlin during the summer of 2023. For information and registration please write to education@hkw.de.

This project is co-conceptualized with Amal Ahaag & André Pitol.

Schattenmuseum
11 June, 9 July Interactive Performance
24 June, 1 July Interactive guided tour with Siri-Box

Performative Game

The *Schattenmuseum* (shadow museum)—composed of thirteen young people ranging in age from eleven to twenty-one who speak a total of six languages—understands itself as an alternative approach to conceptualizing a museum, and as a network it develops proposals to assist institutions in engaging with communities, collections, and educational possibilities. At the O *Quilombismo* exhibition, the *Schattenmuseum* plays with different perspectives, incorporating biographies from the exhibition's artists, from members of the *Schattenmuseum* and their family archives, as well as from street and other interviews. This generates an interactive set-up which is accessible to everyone (ages ten and up) and is offered in German. Visitors are invited to adopt other, new perspectives and engage with 'alien' and fictional biographies and thus move through the game.

Of Resisting and Insisting.
Of Flight as Fight. Of Other
Democratic Egalitarian
Political Philosophies
QUILOMBISMO
HKW
Archive Books
Von Widerstan
Von Flucht als
demokratisch-
Philosophien
HKW

O Quilombismo Reader

This reader, published on the occasion of the project *O Quilombismo*, brings the themes of the eponymous group exhibition to readers interested in wider conceptual explorations around its multifaceted curatorial threads: insurgence, resistance, liberation, spirituality, ecstasy, new cultural forms and aesthetic paradigms, *quilombo* as queering, and the reimagination of collectiveness. Anchored by newly translated historical texts, poetry, essays, and conversations, the publication engages with the founding figures and initial conceptual articulations of *quilombismo* in detail, but also explores how it has found resonance in disparate practices globally.

Contributions by Lillian Allen, Lēnablou, Amanda Carneiro, Jean Casimir, Cosmin Costinaș, Chris Cyrille-Isaac, Paz Guevara, O'Neil Lawrence, Vladimir Lucien, Berette S Macaulay, Jose Ligna Nafafe, Abdias Nascimento, Beatriz Nascimento, Bonaventure Soh Bejeng Ndikung, Marie Helene Pereira, Quỳnh N. Phạm, Carlos Maria Romero aka Atabey, Babalorixá Murah Soares (Ilê Obá Sileké Candomblé Haus in Berlin), Juliana M. Streva, and Eric Otieno Sumba

Publisher: Haus der Kulturen der Welt (HKW) and Archive Books, Berlin, 2023

Approx. 240 pages
Separate German and English editions
Includes 30 images, softcover

ISBN DE: 978-3-949973-27-7
ISBN EN: 978-3-949973-26-0

Price: approx. 26 €

Book launch on Saturday, 3 June, 17:00, see p. 266.

2.6.–9.9.
2023

Sonic Pluriverse Festival

CONGO

Concerts and DJ Sets

Awilo Longomba, Blick Bassy, Estrellas del Caribe, Etuk Ubong & The Etuk Philosophy, Fatoumata Diawara, Mazaher, Nação Zumbi, Oumou Sangaré, Pat Thomas & Kwashibu Area Band

Batila & the DreamBus, Cami Layé Okún, Chrisman (Nyege Nyege), Coco Em, Edna Martinez, Femdelic, Florence Adooni, Ghostpoet, Jembaa Groove, Katerinha & Njeri, La Marimba, La Perla, Makumba (Dengue Dengue Dengue), Mohammad Reza Mortazavi, mokeyanju, MSJY, O.N.A., Sanni Est, SLIC Unit, SNO, among others

Congorama is a sonic inquiry and musical journey across three geographically distant locations sharing unparalleled musical and cultural wealth as well as profound similarities due to transatlantic encounters stemming from their violent colonial pasts and its resonances in the present. From the Congo River—holding in its zigzagging course through the African continent many stories of kingdoms, trade routes, migration, enslavement, colonialism, independence, cultural diversity, creativity, and resistance—through Congo Mirador—a remote floating village in the north of Venezuela, where at times 120 lightning bolts flash across the sky every minute and the spirit of Afro Venezuelan drums beats with them—to Congo Square in New Orleans—a historical gathering place

ORAMA

to develop musical collaborations between enslaved and free people and the birthplace of the cultural music of New Orleans. After the concerts during *Acts of Opening Again*, the festival continues throughout the summer with live music performances, DJ sets, listening sessions, workshops, and lectures. HKW audiences are invited to access traditional, ancestral knowledge, experience rhythm, music, and other sonic practices, and enjoy innovative experiences with a focus on the communal character of how sound connects diverse universes.

Bullerengue

5 June – Franklin Tejedor 'Lamparita', member of Estrellas del Caribe and Mitú

6 June – Bullerengue Circle

2 July – Álvaro Llerena Martínez, son of famous bullerengue *cantadora* Petrona Martínez

30 July – Bullerengue Circle accompanied by the ensemble Mar, Rio y Cordillera

16 September – Bullerengue & Afro-Colombian Dance Practice
Yarley Escudero 'El Happy', Dely Prem

17 September – Emelina Reyes Salgado 'La Burgos', Franklin Hernández 'Lukumí', Yarley Escudero 'El Happy', Dely Prem

Rueda de Bullerengue/Closing of the exhibition – Emelina Reyes Salgado 'La Burgos', Franklin Hernández 'Lukumí', Yarley Escudero 'El Happy', Dely Prem, Bullerengue Circle and participants of the workshops

Series of Music & Dance Workshops

Planting the Seeds for Community Healing

Immediately after the opening weekend, the hosting of communitarian rhythmic cultures by HKW is set in motion. Starting with Afro-Colombian *bullerengue*, Berlin-based members of different migrant communities, feminist, and other advocacy and emancipatory groups are invited to rehearse these *bailes cantados*—sung dances—in a series of workshops accompanied by live drumming, facilitated by artists maintaining this ancestral tradition within their communities. A family of rhythms of West African origin that remains alive in the Colombian Caribbean and the Darién Province in Panama, bullerengue is practised in *ruedas*, or circles, in which participants unify their voices through the repetition of mantra-like choruses that evoke elevation and power. Through a storytelling format of call-and-response, and an improvisatory practice of collective music making and dancing, it activates mutual awareness and a sense of inclusion and belonging. Preserved by elderly women within spaces of intergenerational care and knowledge transmission, bullerengue is founded on forms of spirituality and philosophy used for centuries as tools for healing and resilience. Today, its practice culturally affirms and upholds the histories of resistance rooted in the Afro-diasporic community. There will be drums resonating throughout HKW—join in with clapping, singing, dancing, or playing.

Instruments will be available for rehearsal during the time of the exhibition. Registration and further information at www.hkw.de.

Commissioned and produced by Haus der Kulturen der Welt (HKW), supported by the Embassy of the Republic of Colombia, 2023.

Facilitated by *tamboleros* (drummers), *cantadoras* (singers) and *bailadores* (dancers) from San Basilio de Palenque and Palenque de Chucunate, Turbo, Colombia; co-facilitated and accompanied by the London-based pedagogical project *Bullerengue Circle* (Esteban Card & Valeria Pacific) with monthly online follow-ups and support for music practice.

Acts of Opening Again: A Choreography of Conviviality
2.6.–4.6.2023

Exhibition Opening Times:
Fri 2 June from 17:00–23:00
and Sat 3 & Sun 4 June
from 12:00–23:00

Free admission

O Quilombismo: Of Resisting and Insisting. Of Flight as Fight. Of Other Democratic Egalitarian Political Philosophies
2.6.–17.9.2023

Exhibition Opening Times:
Wed.–Mon. 12:00–19:00

Tickets: €8/€6 reduced

This handbook is included in the price of an exhibition ticket.

Free admission on Mondays and on every first Sunday of the month (Museumssonntag Berlin).

For information on admission to further programmes and events please visit www.hkw.de.

Bookshop opening times:
Wed.–Mon. 12:00–19:00,
extended opening hours during evening programmes.

Restaurant Weltwirtschaft opening times:
Mon.–Fri from 12:00,
weekends from 10:00.
www.weltwirtschaft.berlin

O Quilombismo: Of Resisting and Insisting. Of Flight as Fight. Of Other Democratic Egalitarian Political Philosophies

Exhibition design: Studio Bel Xavier with Claudia Afonso, Alice Schmitx

Guidance system: Studio Yukiko

Haus der Kulturen der Welt (HKW) Team:

Turi Agostino, *Audiovisual Media Engineering*

Philipp Albers, *Editor (Publication Practices)*

Christine Andersen, *Assistance Exhibition Building and Construction*

Hannes Bemm, *Funding Coordinator*

Justus Berger, *Technical Assistance*

Nora Bergreiter, *Project Assistance (Exhibition Practices)*

Emilienne Fernande Bodo, *Curatorial Assistant and Researcher (Architectural and Spatial Practices)*

Lale de Boer, *Student Worker (Music, Performances, and Festivals)*

Pauline Both, *Front Desk*

Dr Sara Morais dos Santos Bruss, *Curator (Scientific, Digital, and Media Practices)*

Julia Büki, *Producer and Researcher (Performative Practices)*

Dr Rosa Cordillera Castillo, *Curator (Discursive Practices)*

René Christoph, *Audiovisual Media Engineering*

Cosmin Costinaş, *Senior Curator (Exhibition Practices)*

Dr Max Czollek, *Visiting Curator*

Jason Dorn, *Event Technician*

Andreas Durchgraf, *Audiovisual Media Engineering*

Alexandra Engel, *General Artistic Operations*

Gernot Ernst, *Head of Exhibition Building and Construction*

Petra Fickinger, *Administrator (Music, Performances, and Festivals)*

Simon Franzkowiak, *Audiovisual Media Engineering*

Júlia Frate Bolliger, *International Press Officer*

Claudia Frenzel, *Assistant to the Director and Chief Curator*

Felix Fuchs, *Student Worker (Exhibition Practices)*

Amaya Gallegos, *Assistant Producer and Researcher (Literature and Oralture Practices)*

Henriette Gallus, *Deputy Director*

Martin Gehrmann, *Exhibition Building and Construction*

Sophie Genske, *Project Assistance (Exhibition Practices)*

Miriam Greiter, *Program Coordinator Schools of Sustainability*

Jakob Grüner, *Trainee (Scientific, Digital, and Media Practices)*

Paz Guevara, *Curator (Exhibition Practices)*

Janne Hagge Ellhöft, *Assistant Communications*

Marco Hanisch, *Assistance Facility Management*

Matthias Hartenberger, *Audiovisual Media Engineering*

Syelle Hase, *Senior Producer and Researcher (Exhibition Practices)*

Tilman Hatje, *Project Coordinator (Exhibition Practices)*

Bastian Heide, *Lighting Technician and Board Operator*

Lilli Heinemann, *Senior Producer and Researcher (Literature and Oralture Practices)*

Ronny Held, *System Administrator Information Technology*

Susanne Held, *Marketing and Finances Officer*

Mathias Helfer, *Technical Director*

Matthias Henkel, *Exhibition Building and Construction*

Eva Hiller, *Administrator (Scientific, Digital, Media, and Discursive Practices)*

Tristan Hinkel, *Front Desk*

Stefan Höhne, *Exhibition Building and Construction*

Henrieke Homburg, *Trainee (Literature and Oralture Practices)*

Frank Jahn, *Head of Facility Management*

Lama El Khatib, *Senior Producer and Researcher (Architectural and Spatial Practices)*

Jan Köhler, *Content Management*

Çiğdem Çağlayan Kolain, *Assistant to the Deputy Director, Program Assistant*

Sabine Krasemann, *Coordinator Controlling Third-Party Funds*

Svetlana Krickovic, *Front Desk*

Matthias Kujawa, *Facility Management*

Ronja Landtau, *Intern (Exhibition Practices and Production)*

Frederick Langkau, *Event Technician*

Elinor Lazar, *Social Media and Press Officer*

Helene Lehrkamp, *Student Worker (Project Funding)*

Marine Lucina, *Producer and Researcher (Cultural Education)*

Dzekashu MacViban, *Curator (Literature and Oralture Practices)*

Marlen Mai, *Student Worker (Documentation Office)*

Virág Major-Kremer, *Producer and Researcher (Scientific, Digital, and Media Practices)*

Edna Martinez, *Curator (Music and Sonic Practices)*

Laura Mattes, *Project Coordination and Partner Projects*

Clara Molau, *Trainee (Press and Marketing)*

Moritz Müller, *Managing Editor (Publication Practices)*

Prof Dr Bonaventure Soh Bejeng Ndikung, *Director and Chief Curator*

Lisa Xenia Ness, *Production Assistant (Exhibition Practices)*

Daniel Neugebauer, *Curator (Cultural Education & Strategic Partnerships)*

Omar Nicolas, *Project Manager Relaunch Mediathek*

Dr Alexandra Ortiz-Wallner, *Curator (Literature and Oralture Practices)*

Jessica Páez, *Senior Producer and Researcher (Performative Practices)*

Carsten Palme, *Facility Management*

Anastasios Papiomytoglou, *Audiovisual Media Engineering*

Marie Helene Pereira, *Senior Curator (Performative Practices)*

Adrian Pilling, *Head of Lighting*

Felix Podzwadowski, *Audiovisual Media Engineering*

Benjamin Pohl, *Head of Event Engineering*

Jan Proest, *Head of Audiovisual Media Engineering*

Veronika Rau, *Senior Producer and Researcher (Literature and Oralture Practices)*

Leonardo Rende, *Lighting Technician and Board Operator*

Lena Katharina Reuter, *Producer and Researcher (Literature and Oralture Practices)*

Carlos Maria Romero aka Atabey, *Curator (Performative Practices)*

Andrew Schmidt, *Exhibition Building and Construction*

Marleen Schröder, *Senior Producer and Researcher (Exhibition Practices)*

Olga Schubert, *Editor (Publication Practices)*

Stefan Seitz, *Exhibition Building and Construction*

Shohreh Shakoory, *Assistant Producer and Researcher (Exhibition Practices)*

Fiona Shipwright, *Assistant Editor (Publication Practices)*

Elisabeth Sinn, *Exhibition Building and Construction*

Muhammed Ali Sözen, *Exhibition Building and Construction*

Dr Sebastian Sprenger, *Overall Production Coordination and Disposition*

Verena Stahl, *Administrator (Literature, Oraltural and Publication Practices)*

Mira Starke, *Coordination Professional Visits*

Eva Stein, *Curator (Cultural Education)*

Goscha Steinhauer, *Project Assistance (Exhibition Practices)*

Merit Steinmeier, *Trainee (Press and Marketing)*

Eric Otieno Sumba, *Editor (Publication Practices)*

Can Sungu, *Curator (Filmic Practices)*

Nicholas Tanton, *Facility Management*

Pia Thilmann, *Producer and Researcher (Festivals)*

Jan Trautmann, *Lead Communications Officer*

Gabriele Tuch, *Senior Producer and Researcher (Festivals, Music, and Special Events)*

Savannah Turner, *Student Worker (Publication Practices)*

Anke Ulrich, *Administrator (Exhibition and Filmic Practices)*

Sophia Vogelsberg, *Project Assistance (Performative Practices)*

Naïma Walter, *Student Worker (Cultural Education)*

Felix Weck, *Audiovisual Media Engineering*

Franziska Wegener, *Managing Editor (Publication Practices)*

Harald Weißmann, *Assistance of the Technical Director / KBB*

Sabine Westemeier, *Database and Invitation Management*

Jill Winder, *Editor (Publication Practices)*

Undine Zamani, *Senior Producer and Researcher (Music and Sonic Practices)*

Kexun Zhang, *Intern (Exhibition Practices)*

Stefan Ziebarth, *Facility Management*

O Quilombismo: Of Resisting and Insisting. Of Flight as Fight. Of Other Democratic Egalitarian Political Philosophies **is funded by the Kulturstiftung des Bundes (German Federal Cultural Foundation).**

The project is funded by

KULTURSTIFTUNG DES BUNDES

In association with the Calouste Gulbenkian Foundation as part of the PARTENARIATS GULBENKIAN programme to support Portuguese and Lusophone art in European artistic institutions.

FONDATION CALOUSTE GULBENKIAN
DÉLÉGATION EN FRANCE

HKW wishes to sincerely thank IPEAFRO / Afro-Brazilian Studies and Research Institute for their collaboration.

O Quilombismo Handbook
is a publication of Haus der Kulturen der Welt (HKW)

Director and Chief Curator: Prof Dr Bonaventure Soh Bejeng Ndikung

Editors: Philipp Albers, Jill Winder

Concept: Henriette Gallus

Managing Editor: Martin Hager

Image Editor: Iris Ströbel

Editorial Assistant: Moritz Müller

Texts: Emilienne Fernande Bodo (EFB), Sara Morais dos Santos Bruss (SM), Rosa Cordillera Castillo (RC), Cosmin Costinaş (CC), Paz Guevara (PG), Dzekashu MacViban (DMV), Edna Martinez (EM), Bonaventure Soh Bejeng Ndikung (BN), Alexandra Ortiz-Wallner (AOW), Marie Helene Pereira (MHP), Carlos Maria Romero aka Atabey (A), Eric Otieno Sumba (EOS), Can Sungu (CS), Jill Winder (JW)

Translation: Colin Shepherd

Copyediting: Fiona Shipwright, Savannah Turner

Design & Layout: Aziza Ahmad, Lilia Di Bella, André Busier, Malin Dittmann, Sina Eggers, Chiara Figone, Yvon Langué for Archive Books

Illustrations: Aziza Ahmad

Printing and Binding: X-PRESS Grafik & Druck, Berlin

Editorial deadline: 17 May 2023
Contents are subject to change.
For the most up-to-date programme, please visit www.hkw.de.

ISBN 978-3-949973-24-6

Archive Books
Reinickendorfer Straße 17
13347 Berlin
Via arquà 15, 20139 Milano
23A Rue OKM 452, Dakar
www.archivebooks.org

Distribution
orders@archivebooks.org

Haus der Kulturen der Welt
John-Foster-Dulles-Allee 10
10557 Berlin
Germany
Tel. +49 (0) 30 397 87 0
Fax +49 (0) 30 394 86 79
info@hkw.de

Haus der Kulturen der Welt is a business division of Kulturveranstaltungen des Bundes in Berlin GmbH.

Director and Chief Curator: Prof Dr Bonaventure Soh Bejeng Ndikung
Managing Director: Charlotte Sieben
Chairwoman of the Supervisory Board: Claudia Roth, Minister of State for Culture and the Media

Haus der Kulturen der Welt is supported by the Minister of State for Culture and the Media as well as by the Federal Foreign Office.

Minister of State for Culture and the Media

Federal Foreign Office

Acts of Opening Again: A Choreography of Conviviality